Contentment of the Heart

By
Shaykh Mufti Saiful Islām

JKN Publications

First Published in May 2019

ISBN 978-1-909114-35-7

British Library Cataloguing in Publication Data
A catalogue record for this book is available from the British Library.

Publisher's Note:

Every care and attention has been put into the production of this book. If however, you find any errors they are our own, for which we seek Allāh ﷻ's forgiveness and reader's pardon.

Published by:

JKN Publications
118 Manningham Lane
Bradford
West Yorkshire
BD8 7JF
United Kingdom

t: +44 (0) 1274 308 456 | w: www.jkn.org.uk | e: info@jkn.org.uk

Book Title: Contentment of the Heart

Author: Shaykh Mufti Saiful Islām

In the Name of Allāh ﷻ, the Most Beneficent, the Most Merciful

Contents

Introduction

All praises are to Allāh ﷻ Who has bestowed the esteemed knowledge of His Dīn upon the hearts of His pious and humble servants. May salutations be upon the last of the Messengers and Prophets - our beloved Prophet Muhammad ﷺ, upon his noble Companions ؓ and upon those who follow their noble lifestyle.

The purification of the soul and its rectification are matters of vital importance which were brought by our Holy Prophet ﷺ to this Ummah. Allāh ﷻ states in Sūrah Āl-Imrān,

لَقَدْ مَنَّ اللَّهُ عَلَى الْمُؤْمِنِينَ إِذْ بَعَثَ فِيهِمْ رَسُولًا مِّنْ أَنفُسِهِمْ يَتْلُو عَلَيْهِمْ آيَاتِهِ وَيُزَكِّيهِمْ وَيُعَلِّمُهُمُ الْكِتَابَ وَالْحِكْمَةَ وَإِن كَانُوا مِن قَبْلُ لَفِي ضَلَالٍ مُّبِينٍ

"Allāh has surely conferred favour upon the believers when He raised in their midst a Messenger from among themselves, reciting to them His verses and purifying them and teaching them the Book and the Wisdom, although earlier they had been in manifest error." (3:164)

The literal meaning of Tazkiyah is 'to cleanse'. The genuine Sūfis assert that the foundation and core of all virtuous character is sincerity and the basis for all evil characteristics and traits is love for this world. The genuine Sūfis emphasised heavily regarding the rectification of the soul and character; they first reformed their own hearts, then steered their associates and disciples towards the same objective. Any type of sin is like poison to the heart which inevitably leads to its annihilation; all diseases of the heart originate from sin-ning. Sin is the impulse which inflames the diseases within the heart. Abdullāh Ibn Mubārak ﷺ quotes, "The person who desires peace, contentment and life for his heart, should purify himself of the poison of sins. It is necessary to constantly monitor the heart, to ensure that it does not falter into sin. If per chance the heart does engage in sin, then he should immediately erase it with Istighfār (sincere repentance) so that the vile and poisonous effects of the sin are cleansed and eliminated. The four poisonous things for the heart are: excessive speech, evil gazes, excessive food and excessive intermingling and socialising. These four things adversely affect the heart and rapidly counteract the life in any heart."

Mālik Ibn Dīnār ﷺ states, "Allāh ﷻ has mercy upon that servant who tells his Nafs that it is worthless, then he belittles and criticizes it until it is subservient to the Holy Qur'ān, to such an extent that the Qur'ān becomes his guide and mentor." It is thus advisable for us as believers to consider it necessary and incumbent to subdue the rantings and evil of this Nafs and not to become frivolous and negligent. Every second of a Muslim's life is precious. The famous Tābi'ī, Hasan Basri ﷺ once mentioned, "Those who take stock of their Nafs in this world will find ease and swiftness in their reckoning on the Day of Judgement. On the other hand, those who are unmindful and careless regarding taking stock of their Nafs in this world, will find difficulty and exertion in their reckoning in the Hereafter.

May Allāh ﷻ accept this work, bless the readers with a purified heart and make us from amongst the closest friends of Allāh ﷻ in this world and the hereafter. May Allāh ﷻ make us all sincere seekers of the True Path and make this book a means of benefit for the masses and the scholars of this Ummah. Āmīn!

(Shaykh Mufti) Saiful Islām
Principal of Jāmiah Khātamun Nabiyeen, Bradford, UK
May 2019/Ramadhān 1440

Part 1

Spiritual Illnesses

نَحْمَدُهُ وَنُصَلِّيْ عَلٰى رَسُوْلِهِ الْكَرِيْمِ

اَمَّا بَعْدُ فَأَعُوْذُ بِاللهِ مِنَ الشَّيْطَانِ الرَّجِيْمِ بِسْمِ اللهِ الرَّحْمٰنِ الرَّحِيْمِ :

يَاۤ اَيُّهَا الَّذِيْنَ اٰمَنُوا اجْتَنِبُوْا كَثِيْرًا مِّنَ الظَّنِّ اِنَّ بَعْضَ الظَّنِّ اِثْمٌ وَّلَا تَجَسَّسُوْا وَلَا يَغْتَبْ بَّعْضُكُمْ بَعْضًا اَيُحِبُّ اَحَدُكُمْ اَنْ يَّأْكُلَ لَحْمَ اَخِيْهِ مَيْتًا فَكَرِهْتُمُوْهُ وَاتَّقُوا اللهَ اِنَّ اللهَ تَوَّابٌ رَّحِيْمٌ

صَدَقَ اللهُ الْعَظِيْمُ

It is of vital importance to remember the reason for why we come to our monthly spiritual gathering; to eradicate, to remove and erase all these spiritual illnesses which we possess within our hearts.

The verse I recited before you in the sermon is from Sūrah Hujurāt. In this Sūrah, Allāh ﷻ mentions many spiritual illnesses which are prevalent within our society and in our environment which we must refrain from and ensure we do not go near them.

Allāh ﷻ firstly addresses the believers by saying,

يَاۤ اَيُّهَا الَّذِيْنَ اٰمَنُوا

"O you who have believed" (49:11)

Sayyidunā Abdullāh Ibn Mas'ūd ﷺ states that whenever Allāh ﷻ us-

10

es the phrase اَلَّذِيْنَ اٰمَنُوْا, we as believers must listen attentively because Allāh ﷻ is directly referring to us. In the Holy Qur'ān, when Allāh ﷻ says, "يَاۤاَيُّهَاالنَّاسُ O people/mankind" He is referring to mankind as an entirety. However, when Allāh ﷻ says, يَاۤاَيُّهَا الَّذِيْنَ اٰمَنُوْا - He is expressing the special bond/relationship between Himself and His servants who are truly obedient.

In this particular verse, Allāh ﷻ mentions various spiritual illnesses and explains that the main root and problem due to which all these various spiritual illnesses occur is suspicion.

First Spiritual Illness

Firstly Allāh ﷻ says,

يَاۤاَيُّهَا الَّذِيْنَ اٰمَنُوْا اجْتَنِبُوْا كَثِيْرًا مِّنَ الظَّنِّ اِنَّ بَعْضَ الظَّنِّ اِثْمٌ

"O you who believe, save yourselves from excessive suspicion because verily certain suspicions are sins." (49:12)

There are different types of suspicion. Here, Allāh ﷻ says that some types of suspicions are sins. Those suspicions which one does not hold any concrete evidence for are sinful. For example, merely having a negative assumption regarding a Muslim brother or sister is completely forbidden.

11

<u>Types of Suspicion</u>

Imām Abū Bakr Jassās ﷺ mentions in one of his notable works, Ahkāmul Qur'ān that there are four different types of ظَنّ (assumption):

1.   To possess ill thoughts regarding Allāh ﷻ is Harām. To think Allāh ﷻ will commit injustice, oppression or tyranny is completely wrong.

The Hadīth of the Holy Prophet ﷺ states,

$$لَا يَمُوْتَنَّ أَحَدُكُمْ إِلَّا وَهُوَ يُحْسِنُ الظَّنَّ بِاللهِ عَزَّ وَجَلَّ$$

"Let not one of you (believers) die unless you have good thoughts concerning Allāh ﷻ." (Muslim)

A person's level of Imān should be kept between fear and hope, but when one is leaving this world, one should have more hope than fear.

When the great Imām, Imām Ahmad Ibn Hanbal ﷺ was leaving this world, he called his son Abdullāh and requested, "O my beloved son! Recite the Ahādīth which are pertaining to the mercy of Allāh ﷻ; I want to have good thoughts with regards to Allāh ﷻ whilst I am leaving this world." His son therefore recited those relevant Ahādīth and in that state, Imām Ahmad Ibn Hanbal ﷺ left this world.

2. To maintain good thoughts with regards to Allāh ﷻ is compulsory. To think Allāh ﷻ will exhibit justice and will express and descend His mercy and tranquillity upon His servants is necessary.

The Hadīth Qudsī mentions,

اَنَا عِنْدَ ظَنِّ عَبْدِيْ بِيْ

"I am with My servant's thoughts." (Bukhāri)

In this Hadīth, Allāh ﷻ is explaining that if His servant thinks good concerning Him, He will think good regarding him. However, if His servant thinks bad concerning Him, He will think bad with regards to him.

3. Similarly, to possess ill thoughts regarding any of the believers without a genuine excuse or without any concrete evidence is completely impermissible.

When a group of people held negative thoughts about Sayyidah Ā'ishah ﷞ with regards to the incident of اِفْك (slander) - certain Companions ﷢ assumed that our beloved mother Sayyidah Ā'ishah ﷞ committed adultery. In response to the false allegation, Allāh ﷻ revealed the following verses,

لَوْلَا إِذْ سَمِعْتُمُوهُ ظَنَّ الْمُؤْمِنُونَ وَالْمُؤْمِنَاتُ بِأَنْفُسِهِمْ خَيْرًا وَّقَالُوا هٰذَا إِفْكٌ مُّبِيْنٌ

13

"Why, when you (O believers) heard of it, did the believing men and the believing women not think good of one another and (why did they not) say, 'This is a manifest lie.' (24:12)

إِنَّ الَّذِينَ يُحِبُّونَ أَن تَشِيعَ الْفَاحِشَةُ فِي الَّذِينَ آمَنُوا لَهُمْ عَذَابٌ أَلِيمٌ فِي الدُّنْيَا وَالْآخِرَةِ وَاللَّهُ يَعْلَمُ وَأَنتُمْ لَا تَعْلَمُونَ

"Indeed, those who like that immorality/lewdness should be spread among those who have believed, for them there is painful punishment in the world and the hereafter. And Allāh knows and you do not know." (24:19)

Allāh ﷻ says if one thinks bad about their Muslim brother or sister, it is as if one is thinking bad about ones own self. The word بِأَنفُسِهِم in the verse refers to 'your own selves'.

Regarding this incident, when Sayyidunā Abū Ayyūb Ansāri ﷺ came home and his wife asked, "Have you heard about Ā'ishah?!" Immediately, Sayyidunā Abū Ayyūb Ansāri ﷺ replied, "It is false and a manifest lie." His wife asked, "How do you know?" Sayyidunā Abū Ayyūb Ansāri ﷺ replied, "If somebody said that about you, would I accept it!?" His wife replied, "No!" Sayyidunā Abū Ayyūb Ansāri ﷺ said, "How can this be then accepted regarding the daughter of Abū Bakr? How can this be thought about regarding the beloved wife of the Holy Prophet ﷺ?"

This is the attitude we should have about our fellow Muslim brothers and sisters. Unfortunately, in our society, we will take the bad thoughts on board, promote it and send messages on social media to see that this person is totally disgraced. This is something for us to learn from! Thus, it is necessary for us to have good thoughts about our Muslim brothers and sisters and it is Harām to have ill thoughts about our Muslim brothers and sisters.

To act according to the assumption in Salāh is permissible. For example, one is performing Salāh and within Salāh, a doubt occurs as to whether one has performed three or four Rak'ats. In this situation it is permissible for one to take a whole figure: three or four. The scholars have said it is permissible for the person to go according to certainty of three Rak'ats or the stronger assumption of four Rak'ats.

Within our daily lives, we utilise our ظَنُ. For example, when a case is presented in front of the judge, the judge does not have full certainty, hence he demands the participants to take an oath or present witnesses. The judge is not certain as to whether the witnesses are true or false - the assessment is done through ظَنُ.

The Holy Prophet ﷺ has said,

$$\text{اَلْبَيِّنَةُ عَلَى الْمُدَّعِي وَالْيَمِيْنُ عَلَى مَنْ أَنْكَرَ}$$

"The burden of proof is on the accuser and swearing the oath is on the one accused." (Baihaqī)

15

4.   To keep good thoughts in general with regards to the believers is Mustahab. If one enquires regarding a certain Muslim brother or sister, the reply should be that they are good. For instance, if a person is seen going to the Masjid and somebody asks another as to whether this person is good, the reply should be, "Māshā-Allāh, he is going towards the Masjid. I have good thoughts about him." A person going to the Masjid itself is an evidence that this person is good.

The Holy Prophet ﷺ has said,

إِذَا رَأَيْتُمُ الرَّجُلَ يَتَعَاهَدُ الْمَسْجِدَ فَاشْهَدُوا لَهُ بِالْإِيمَانِ فَإِنَّ اللهَ تَعَالَى يَقُوْلُ إِنَّمَا يَعْمُرُ مَسَاجِدَ اللهِ مَنْ أَمَنَ بِاللهِ وَالْيَوْمِ الْأَخِرِ وَأَقَامَ الصَّلَاةَ وَأَتَى الزَّكَاةَ وَلَمْ يَخْشَ إِلَّا اللهَ فَعَسَى أُوْلِئِكَ أَنْ يَّكُوْنُوا مِنَ الْمُهْتَدِيْنَ

"When you see a person frequenting the Masjid, give the witness that he is a believer. Indeed, Allāh ﷻ says, "The Houses of Allāh are only to be maintained by those who believe in Allāh, the Last Day, establish Salāh, give Zakāt and who fear none but Allāh. It is hoped that those will be of the rightly guided (9:18) ." (Tirmizi)

The Holy Prophet ﷺ has said,

إِيَّاكُمْ وَالظَّنَّ فَإِنَّ الظَّنَّ أَكْذَبُ الْحَدِيْثِ

"Save yourself from bad suspicions because indeed having bad suspicions is the worst type of lies." (Bukhāri, Muslim)

In conclusion, if we are to hold any negative suspicions or assumptions with regards to our Muslim brothers or sisters, then this will ultimately lead us to start looking for faults.

Second Spiritual Illness

After suspicion and assumption, spying takes place. Subsequently, Allāh ﷻ mentions the second spiritual illness,

وَلَا تَجَسَّسُوْا

"And do not spy/be curious (to find out the faults of others)." (49:12)

The Hadīth of the Holy Prophet ﷺ states,

إِيَّاكُمْ وَالظَّنَّ فَإِنَّ الظَّنَّ أَكْذَبُ الْحَدِيْثِ وَلَا تَحَسَّسُوْا وَلَاتَجَسَّسُوْا وَلَا تَنَافَسُوْا وَلَا تَحَاسَدُوْا وَلَا تَبَاغَضُوْا وَلَا تَقَاطَعُوْا وَلَا تَدَابَرُوْا وَكُوْنُوْا عِبَادَ اللهِ إِخْوَانًا

"Save yourselves from suspicion because suspicion is the worst type of lie, do not start to find faults within each other, do not spy, do not envy each other, do not be jealous of each other, do not have hatred for one another, do not sever relationships, do not show your back to one another (i.e. do not turn away from each other) and become the servants of Allāh ﷻ as brothers." (Bukhārī, Muslim)

There are two words within the Arabic language:

1. وَلَا تَجَسَّسُوْا

2. وَلَا تَحَسَّسُوْا

The word تَجَسُّس refers to searching for people's secrets and spying on people's secrets. In this current era, it refers to listening to people's private phone calls, overhearing private conversations with the latest gadgets etc.

The word تَحَسُّس refers to general searching. It can have an evil connotation as well as a good connotation. Allāh ﷻ mentions in the Holy Qur'ān that Sayyidunā Ya'qūb عليه السلام said,

يَٰبَنِيَّ اذْهَبُوْا فَتَحَسَّسُوْا مِنْ يُّوْسُفَ وَأَخِيْهِ وَلَا تَيْأَسُوْا مِنْ رَّوْحِ اللهِ إِنَّهُ لَا يَيْأَسُ مِنْ رَّوْحِ اللهِ إِلَّا الْقَوْمُ الْكَافِرُوْنَ

"O my sons, go and search for Yūsuf and his brother and do not lose hope in the mercy of Allāh. Indeed, only the disbelieving people lose hope in Allāh's mercy." (12:87)

In this context, the word تَحَسُّس refers to a general search and has a good connotation.

How beautifully Allāh ﷻ mentions,

إِنَّمَا الْمُؤْمِنُونَ إِخْوَةٌ فَأَصْلِحُوا بَيْنَ أَخَوَيْكُمْ وَاتَّقُوا اللهَ لَعَلَّكُمْ تُرْحَمُونَ

"All believers are but brothers, therefore seek reconciliation between your brothers and fear Allāh so that you may receive mercy." (49:10)

Unfortunately in this day and age, we constantly have hatred for each other. This is completely contrary to the love and affection Sūrah Hujurāt is teaching us to adopt.

Mirror of a Believer

How amazingly the Holy Prophet ﷺ says in a Hadīth,

اَلْمُؤْمِنُ مِرْآةُ الْمُؤْمِنِ

"A believer is a mirror of another believer." (Tabarāni)

We need to ponder over this Hadīth carefully. Many a times when we go in front of the mirror, we do not really think about it. We should not just say, "Mirror, mirror on the wall, who is the fairest of them all?!" When we truly think deep regarding this Hadīth of the Holy Prophet ﷺ, we will come to realise that a mirror is not just a mirror.

Why did the Holy Prophet ﷺ use the similitude of a mirror? It is amazing how the scholars have explained, expounded and elucidated upon these points within this similitude and parable.

Number 1:

اِنَّ الْمُؤْمِنَ يُرِي أَخَاهُ عُيُوبَهُ الَّتِي لَا يُمْكِنُه أَنْ يَّرَاهَا مِنْ نَفْسِه كَمَا اِنَّ كَثِيْرًا مِّنْ أَعْضَاءِ الْجَسَدِ وَعُيُوبَ الْبَدَنِ لَا يُمْكِنُ رُؤْيَتُهَا إِلَّا بِالْمِرْآةِ

فَيُعَلِّمُكَ أَخُوْكَ الْمُؤْمِنُ إِذَا جَهِلْتَ وَيُذَكِّرُكَ إِذَا نَسِيْتَ وَيُنَبِّهُكَ إِذَا غَفَلْتَ وَيُصَوِّبُكَ إِذَا أَخْطَأْتَ

A believer shows his brother his faults which he usually cannot see himself. Likewise, many parts of the body and faults of the body are not visible without the assistance of a mirror. Just as a mirror will display the individual their faults, a true believer will teach his Mu'min brother when he is ignorant. He will remind his brother when he forgets, he will inform him and direct him when he becomes heedless and he will guide him when he errs.

Number 2:

وَالْمِرْآةُ صَادِقَةٌ فِيْمَا تُعَكِّسُه مِنْ هَيْئَتِكَ وَكَذٰلِكَ الْمُؤْمِنُ يُرِيْكَ حَسَنَاتِكَ وَيَشْكُرُكَ عَلَيْهَا وَيُرِيْكَ سَيِّئَاتِكَ وَيُنَبِّهُكَ إِلَيْهَا

A mirror will tell you the exact truth and will reflect exactly the same truth. Likewise, a true believer will show his brother his good qualities as well as his faults; he will not compromise. Therefore a true believer will show his Mu'min brother his good qualities and he will express his gratitude upon them. If he perceives a good trait of his brother he will tell him just like a mirror.

For example, an individual has got a good, fit, healthy body and possesses biceps etc but at the same time, he is unfortunately bald. The mirror will not compromise and say, "Just hide the bald patches, you are okay." No! It will show and reflect every defect in the truthful way. The mirror will display the good and the bad. Likewise, a true believer will say to his brother, Māshā-Allāh, you have got all these good qualities but simultaneously, you just need to improve in these certain areas. A true believer will teach his brother and not disgrace him.

Number 3:

وَهُوَ يُرِيْهِ عُيُوْبَهُ كَمَا هِيَ دُوْنَ تَهْوِيْلٍ أَوْ تَضْخِيْمٍ

The mirror will show the person exactly the way they are without any exaggeration. Likewise, a true believer will show his Mu'min brother his faults as it appears, not making flattering comments such as, "O' Hazrat Allāmah Sāhib". The mirror will not exaggerate like this.

If a person has a spot on their left cheek, the mirror will not show another scar on the right cheek. If a person has one spot, it will not show three spots. In the same way, if a Muslim brother has got one mistake, a true believer will not say he has got so many mistakes. He will just say exactly what and how many mistakes he may have.

Number 4:

إِنَّ الْمِرْآةَ صَامِتَةٌ تُرِ يْكَ مَا فِيْ بَدَنِكَ كَمَا هِيَ

Indeed the mirror is quiet. It will silently display exactly what is on the body. A mirror will not yell and scream, "O you have these faults in you!" It will politely and softly inform a person. These are all amazing points of how the similitude is given. These are the qualities we should aspire to obtain regarding our fellow Muslim brothers and sisters.

Number 5:

إِذَا ابْتَعَدْتَ عَنِ الْمِرْآةِ زَالَتْ صُوْرَتُكَ وَهٰكَذَا الْمُؤْمِنُ إِذَا انْطَلَقَ كَتَمَ سِرَّكَ

When one moves away from the mirror, the mirror erases the individual's identity. Likewise, when a true believer goes away, he hides his brother's secret.

It will never occur that after a person has gone away from the mirror, it will say to another person, "O the previous person who came in front of me was so obese, so evil, so ugly." The mirror will never re-veal to the other person what it actually saw. Correspondingly, when a brother leaves after having been given advice, a true believer will not say, "O' this person who came before was like this." He will not divulge any negative information to the next client, brother or sister.

Number 6:

إِنَّ الْمِرْآةَ مِنْ أَهَمِّ وَسَائِلِ الزِّيْنَةِ بَلْ لَا يَكَادُ يَتِمُّ التَّزَيُّنُ إِلَّا بِهَا

Indeed the mirror is one of the most important tools of beautifica-tion. If an individual wishes to beautify themself, they will always use a mirror.

A person will enquire and ask his Muslim brother, "How am I broth-er? Is everything okay? What faults can you see in me?" A true be-liever will inform and advise his Muslim brother for example, if they are embarking on a journey, he will advise him that he should keep such and such points in his mind, these are the things to look into, these are the things he needs to keep away from.

A person is in need of a mirror all the time in order to beautify him-self. Likewise, in the same way, a believer needs his brother in order to beautify himself in terms of Akhlāq (character).

Number 7:

اِنَّ الْمِرْآةَ لَا تَطَّلِعُ إِلَّا عَلَى الظَّاهِرِ فَلَا سَبِيْلَ لَهَا إِلَى الْبَاطِنِ وَهٰكَذَا الْمُؤْمِنُ يُعَامِلُ أَخَاهُ بِظَاهِرِهِ وَلَا يَطْعَنَ فِيْ بَاطِنِه

Indeed a mirror only shows the apparent things (the external things), it does not have access to the internal side. In a similar manner, a true believer will only deal with the external things and will not taunt or tease his brother pertaining to his internal state.

For example, one has offered Salām to his brother and he replies, "No, he is not sincere in offering his Salām," or a person comes and gives charity and you say, "I do not think he was sincere in giving." No! A Muslim is a mirror for another believer; not an x-ray machine! We are not obliged to look into an individual's personal or internal matter like an x-ray machine.

In the Holy Prophet's ﷺ use of the word 'mirror', have we ever thought of all these intricacies? Next time, when looking into a mirror, let us look deep into it and ponder over these aforementioned points; we should not just have a casual look. Why did the Holy Prophet ﷺ use this similitude? If we can deeply ponder over this, all the sins which we perpetrate (for example suspicion, spying etc.) will be eradicated.

Third Spiritual Illness

When a person begins to spy, they may find a defect present within somebody which will prompt them to start backbiting or even slander. Regarding the third spiritual illness, Allāh ﷻ states,

وَلَا يَغْتَب بَّعْضُكُم بَعْضًا أَيُحِبُّ أَحَدُكُمْ أَن يَأْكُلَ لَحْمَ أَخِيهِ مَيْتًا فَكَرِهْتُمُوهُ

"Do not backbite one another. Does one of you like that he eats the flesh of his dead brother? You would abhor it." (49:12)

The word غَابَ يَغِيبُ literally means somebody who is not present. Backbiting is thus talking about somebody who is not in your presence.

A Companion ؓ asked the Holy Prophet ﷺ, "If we were talking about an individual who is absent, however, it is a true fact about that person, is this backbiting?" The Holy Prophet ﷺ replied,

اِنْ كَانَ فِيْهِ مَا تَقُوْلُ فَقَدِ اغْتَبْتَهُ وَاِنْ لَّمْ يَكُنْ فِيْهِ فَقَدْ بَهَتَّه

"If the habit is present in the individual then this is backbiting. If this habit is not in that individual, then indeed you have slandered him." (Muslim)

In this day and age, it is not only backbiting, we go one step further and make up things about a person and spread that rumour. This is slandering, which is worse than backbiting. Backbiting is so dangerous and has become the social norm; nearly every gathering has backbiting present within it.

The Holy Prophet ﷺ has said,

لَا تَغْتَابُوا الْمُسْلِمِيْنَ وَلَا تَتَّبِعُوْا عَوْرَاتِهِمْ فَإِنَّهُ مَنِ اتَّبَعَ عَوْرَاتِهِمْ يَتَّبِعِ اللهُ عَوْرَتَهُ وَمَنْ يَّتَّبِعِ اللهُ عَوْرَتَهُ يَفْضَحْهُ فِيْ بَيْتِهِ

"Do not backbite the believers. Do not start to look at the faults of the believers. Allāh ﷻ will look into the faults of the person who looks for the faults of the believers. Whosoever's faults Allāh ﷻ looks into, Allāh ﷻ will disgrace that person within his own house." (Abū Dāwūd)

Harms of Backbiting

In the verse,

وَلَا يَغْتَبْ بَّعْضُكُمْ بَعْضًا أَيُحِبُّ أَحَدُكُمْ أَنْ يَّأْكُلَ لَحْمَ أَخِيْهِ مَيْتًا فَكَرِهْتُمُوْهُ

"Do not backbite one another. Does one of you like that he eats the flesh of his dead brother? You would abhor it." (49:12)

Allāh ﷻ makes mention of eating the flesh of a dead brother, not of eating the flesh of one who is alive. The reason is because Allāh ﷻ is saying that this person whom you are backbiting about is not in your presence hence it is like eating their dead flesh.

If one was to eat the flesh of a person who is dead, the dead person would not receive any physical pain. In the same way, when a person is backbiting against another person, that individual is not receiving any pain at that time. However, it is very inhumane to do that. The reverse scenario is when a person is finding faults, ridiculing and insulting a Muslim brother or sister in their presence. This is as if the person is eating the flesh of his brother/sister who is alive. If an individual is insulting or ridiculing another person in their presence, the person who is being ridiculed is able to defend themself.

However, when people talk with regards to a person in their absence, there maybe nobody there to defend this person. Many a times, people who are sitting around and listening, enjoy backbiting and will not want to defend that person.

Sayyidunā Maymūn ﷺ narrates an incident in which he says that he saw a dream. In the dream, he heard a voice saying to him, "Go and eat the flesh of this African person." He asked as to why he should go and eat the flesh of this African person. The voice said to him, "You have committed backbiting." He replied in the negative and said he did not commit backbiting. The voice said that he had been in a gathering in which backbiting was committed and he was listening to it. When one listens to backbiting, this is equivalent to backbiting.

Sayyidunā Maymūn ﷺ immediately awoke and took extra precaution to ensure he never backbites anyone and also, whenever somebody was backbiting, he would instantly stop them or he would move away from that gathering. We need to really reflect and think as to how we can eradicate these spiritual illnesses which we have within ourselves.

Sayyidunā Anas ؓ narrates that when the Holy Prophet ﷺ went on the journey of Mi'rāj, he saw a group of people who had long fingernails made of copper. The group were scratching their faces and chests with their fingernails. The Holy Prophet ﷺ asked Sayyidunā Jibrīl عليه السلام as to who these people were. Sayyidunā Jibrīl عليه السلام replied that these were the people from the Holy Prophet's ﷺ nation who used to backbite. The Holy Prophet ﷺ once said,

$$\text{اَلْغِيْبَةُ أَشَدُّ مِنَ الزِّنَا}$$

"Backbiting is worse than unlawful intercourse." (Baihaqī)
The Sahābah ؓ were shocked and asked the Holy Prophet ﷺ as to how backbiting could be worse than unlawful intercourse. The Holy Prophet ﷺ replied, when a person commits Zinā (unlawful intercourse), they feel guilty and remorseful, thus, immediately they repent to Allāh ﷻ or Allāh ﷻ grants them the ability to repent. However, when a person is backbiting, a person does not realise that they have committed a sin and thus, they are reluctant to go to the person they have backbitten to ask for forgiveness.

The rights of the servants of Allāh ﷻ will not be forgiven until that person forgives - this is a general ruling.

<u>Ruling of Backbiting</u>

If a person has committed backbiting, the ruling is as follows:

* If a person is certain that this negative information which has been said regarding another individual has been narrated to that individual and is abusive, or will tarnish their reputation or honour, then a person must seek forgiveness from that specific individual.

* If a person knows that this negative information has not yet been narrated to the person, it is best not to convey that information. Rather, a person should do Istighfār (ask for forgiveness) for himself and that person.

It has been narrated by Imām Baihaqī ﷺ that the Holy Prophet ﷺ has said,

اِنَّ مِنْ كَفَّارَةِ الْغِيْبَةِ اَنْ تَسْتَغْفِرَ لِمَنِ اغْتَبْتَهٗ تَقُوْلُ اَللّٰهُمَّ اغْفِرْ لَنَا وَلَه

"The atonement for backbiting is that one does Istighfār (asks for forgiveness) for the individual who he has backbitten against by saying, "O' Allāh, forgive us and forgive him.""

Whilst reciting the Du'ā, اَللّٰهُمَّ اغْفِرْ لَنَا وَلَه, when a person reaches the word وَلَه (and for him), the person who was backbitten against i.e. the individual's name, can be mentioned or if a gathering was back-

29

bitten against, all the names can be mentioned.

We need to ensure that we constantly repent and do Istighfār for ourselves and for our Muslim brothers and sisters. In this way, we can move forward and eradicate these spiritual illnesses. If we wish to rectify our hearts, one main spiritual illness we need to take out is jealousy from our hearts as jealousy breeds the rest of the spiritual illnesses.

The Holy Prophet ﷺ once advised Sayyidunā Anas Ibn Mālik ﷺ,

يَا بُنَيَّ إِنْ قَدَرْتَ أَنْ تُصْبِحَ وَتُمْسِيَ وَ لَيْسَ فِيْ قَلْبِكَ غِشٌّ لِأَحَدٍ فَافْعَلْ ثُمَّ قَالَ لِيْ يَا بُنَيَّ وَذٰلِكَ مِنْ سُنَّتِيْ وَمَنْ أَحَبَّ سُنَّتِيْ فَقَدْ أَحَبَّنِيْ وَمَنْ أَحَبَّنِيْ كَانَ مَعِيْ فِي الْجَنَّةِ

"O my beloved son, if you can spend your morning and evening in this state that you do not have hatred, jealousy, or enmity regarding your Muslim brother then do that. O my beloved son, this is from my Sunnah; whosoever loves my Sunnah, loves me and whosoever loves me will be with me in Paradise." (Tirmizi)

We tend to think that Sunnah refers to using the Miswāk, putting on the turban etc. - All these are from the external Sunnats. However, these are the internal Sunnats which are much more important in order for us to eradicate all these evil habits and spiritual maladies from our hearts.

Atonement for Backbiting

If a person is in a gathering and has said something negative about an individual, there are two ways in which the person can atone their mistake:

1. In the gathering, a person needs to retract their statement. The person who had backbitten somebody should confess in the gathering that whatever was said was completely wrong.
2. A person should praise the person who they had backbitten in future gatherings.

Backbiting in general is Harām (forbidden). Backbiting regarding minor (small) children and non-Muslims is Harām as well. Backbiting does not have to be verbal; it can be through indication as well. For example, if one sees a person and he indicates, winks or sticks his tongue out etc to show that the individual is short or overweight, this will also be categorised as backbiting. Even writing or typing insulting words on social media is classed as backbiting.

In the farewell Hajj, the Holy Prophet ﷺ said,

فَإِنَّ دِمَاءَكُمْ وَأَمْوَالَكُمْ وَأَعْرَاضَكُمْ بَيْنَكُمْ حَرَامٌ كَحُرْمَةِ يَوْمِكُمْ هٰذَا فِيْ شَهْرِكُمْ هٰذَا فِيْ بَلَدِكُمْ هٰذَا

"Indeed your blood, your wealth and your honour is sanctified like this day is sanctified (the day of Arafāt) in this month of yours (Dhul Hijjah) and in this place of yours (Makkah Mukarramah)." (Bukhāri)

31

In the way the day of Arafāt, Dhul Hijjah and Makkah Mukarramah are sacred, similarly to a higher degree, the blood, wealth and honour of a Muslim is sacred.

<u>Permissibility of Backbiting</u>

Backbiting only becomes permissible in dire necessity or in exceptional cases. For example, if a person is being oppressive towards you, you can go to the ruler, king, president etc. and complain regarding him and say this person is committing injustice against you. Hence, a person can go to a higher authority in order to defend themself.

If a wife is being troubled by her husband and the rights are not being fulfilled, she may go to a Mufti or a judge and complain that her husband does not fulfil her rights and does not provide accommodation for her. This may be apparently backbiting, but in order to acquire an Islamic ruling it is permissible.

It is permissible for the Imām or leader to warn and inform the Muslim community regarding a person who is very evil, openly commits sins or is a drug dealer, thief etc.

Another example is if a person comes to take advice and says they would like to do a business partnership with a certain person. However, from experience you know that this person is very devious, cheats and is a liar. In such a circumstance it can be said, "I have dealt with him, so do not deal with him."

The individual should have a true and genuine intention of informing their Muslim brother so that they do not fall into any kind of trouble. It cannot be done for any personal reasons as the Holy Prophet ﷺ has said,

$$لَا يُلْدَغُ الْمُؤْمِنُ مِنْ جُحْرٍ وَاحِدٍ مَرَّتَيْنِ$$
"A believer is not bitten from the same hole twice."
(Bukhārī, Muslim)

Question: If a person says, I have put forward a proposal for my daughter to this particular person, what is your opinion about this person? Is it permissible to backbite about them?

Answer: If an individual knows about this person, it is permissible to give sincere advice by backbiting. The intention should not be to take revenge or expose their faults.

It has been narrated by Imām Muslim ﷺ that a female Companion came to the Holy Prophet ﷺ and told him that two proposals have come to her - one from Sayyidunā Muāwiyah ﷺ and the other from Sayyidunā Abū Jahm ﷺ. She asked him which she should accept. The Holy Prophet ﷺ replied, "Muāwiyah is a very poor person. (In the beginning stages of Islām, Sayyidunā Muāwiyah ﷺ was very poor.) And Abū Jahm is very harsh towards women." The Holy

Prophet ﷺ provided the true information and explained the situation.

The Pious Predecessors

Besides the aforementioned scenarios, backbiting is not allowed. Imām Bukhāri ﷺ once said, "The day I realised backbiting is Harām, I never committed backbiting." Hakīmul Ummah, Shaykh Ashraf Ali Thānwi ﷺ says, "To refrain from backbiting, one should not mention anything regarding a person who is not present in the gathering." Shaytān works in many strange ways and the person will say, "This person is very good BUT...". This 'but' commences the backbiting.

When Sayyidunā Uqbah Ibn Āmir ﷺ met the Holy Prophet ﷺ, he asked: "What is نجاة (salvation)?" The Holy Prophet ﷺ beautifully answered,

$$ أَمْلِكْ عَلَيْكَ لِسَانَكَ وَلْيَسَعْكَ بَيْتُكَ وَابْكِ عَلَى خَطِيْئَتِكَ $$

"Restrain your tongue, let your house be sufficient for you (i.e. do not go out of your house unnecessarily) and cry upon your sins." (Musnad Ahmad)

Maulānā Ya'qūb Nānotwi ﷺ mentions the way our pious predecessors would control their tongues. He mentions that they would write down all the words they had uttered during that day and would scrutinise each sentence and each word and would deeply ponder whether this (certain phrase or sentence) was necessary to say or not.

The Hadīth of the Holy Prophet ﷺ states,

مَنْ كَانَ يُؤْمِنُ بِاللهِ وَالْيَوْمِ الْأَخِرِ فَلْيَقُلْ خَيْرًا أَوْ لِيَصْمُتْ

"Whoever has faith in Allāh ﷻ and the Last Day should either speak what is good or remain silent." (Bukhāri, Muslim).

If a person has nothing beneficial to say, the person should stay quiet. Unfortunately, we wish to say anything and everything. With our mobile phones, we just carry on talking, texting etc. and do not realize .

After mentioning the spiritual maladies, Allāh ﷻ says,

وَاتَّقُوا اللَّهَ إِنَّ اللَّهَ تَوَّابٌ رَّحِيمٌ

"Fear Allāh! Surely Allāh is Most accepting of repentance, Most Merciful." (49:12)

After committing these sins, a person should not be despondent as Allāh ﷻ says, He is the most accepting of repentance. The word تَوَّابٌ is a superlative noun. Whenever the word تَوَّابٌ comes with the word Allāh ﷻ, it means Allāh ﷻ is forgiving and accepts repentance.

Whenever the word تَوَّابٌ comes with a human being, it means a person who repents a lot.

Allāh ﷻ is also رَحِيْمٌ (Merciful). Again this word is also a superlative noun which means Allāh ﷻ is the Most Merciful.

Four Meanings of Mercy

In Bayānul Qur'ān, Hakīmul Ummah, Shaykh Ashraf Ali Thānwi ﷫ mentions that whenever we ask Allāh ﷻ to shower His divine mercy upon us, we should keep four things in mind:

1. We should ask Allāh ﷻ for توفيق طاعة - the ability to carry out acts of obedience. Due to excessive sinning, we are deprived of the ability to carry out acts of obedience. By saying وَارْحَمْنَا we are asking Allāh ﷻ to bestow His divine mercy in giving us back the ability to carry out good deeds again.

2. We should ask Allāh ﷻ for فراخي معيشت - expansion of sustenance. Due to excessive sinning, we are deprived from sustenance. By saying وَارْحَمْنَا we ask Allāh ﷻ to show mercy in order to obtain expansion in our sustenance after it has been constricted because of our sins.

The Holy Prophet ﷺ said,

إِنَّ الرَّجُلَ لَيُحْرَمُ الرِّزْقَ بِالذَّنْبِ يُصِيبُه

"Indeed a person is deprived from sustenance because of the sins he commits." (Ibn Mājah)

3.   We should ask Allāh ﷻ for مغفرت بے حساب - forgiveness without reckoning.

The Holy Prophet ﷺ once said,

مَنْ نُّوقِشَ عُذِّبَ

"A person who is taken to account will be punished." (Bukhāri)

Sayyidah Ā'ishah ﷺ replied, "Did the Qur'ān not say:

فَأَمَّا مَنْ أُوتِيَ كِتَابَهُ بِيَمِينِه فَسَوْفَ يُحَاسَبُ حِسَابًا يَّسِيرًا

"So, as for him whose book of deeds will be given to him in his right hand, he will be judged with an easy account."(84:7-8)

The Holy Prophet ﷺ replied that this is merely with regards to presenting. If an examiner already has the intention of passing a student, they will merely look at the paper and say that this individual has passed. If an examiner wishes to scrutinise the paper, he will be harsh and the student is unlikely to pass. If Allāh ﷻ wishes to admit a person into Jannah, Allāh ﷻ will not inspect the person's book of deeds. By saying وَارْحَمْنَا we ask Allāh ﷻ to show mercy by not taking us to task.

4.   We should ask Allāh ﷻ for دخول جنة - entry into Jannah. Due to excessive sinning, we are deprived of entry into Jannah—the ultimate place of Rahmah (mercy) as we do not have any deeds worthy of presenting in front of Allāh ﷻ. By saying وَارْحَمْنَا we ask Allāh ﷻ to shower His divine mercy upon us so we can be admitted into Jannah where the complete mercy of Allāh ﷻ will be displayed.

The Holy Prophet ﷺ said,

اَلتَّائِبُ مِنَ الذَّنْبِ كَمَنْ لَا ذَنْبَ لَه

"The one who repents from sins is like the one who has no sins." (Ibn Mājah)

كُلُّ بَنِي آدَمَ خَطَّاءٌ وَخَيْرُ الْخَطَّائِينَ التَّوَّابُونَ

"The children of Ādam are all wrongdoers, but the best of the wrong-doers are those who repent." (Tirmizi)

Out of the three spiritual illnesses, the conclusion is that the root of all these illnesses is suspicion, hence each one of these illnesses have a domino effect.

By stopping and eradicating the illness of suspicion, it will stop a person from spying and backbiting. Allāh ﷻ mentions,

وَلَا تَقْرَبُوا الزِّنَا إِنَّهُ كَانَ فَاحِشَةً وَسَآءَ سَبِيلًا

"Do not even go close to fornication. It is indeed a shameful act and an evil way to follow." (17:32)

Allāh ﷻ did not say لَا تَفْعَلُوا which means do not commit. Allāh ﷻ used the word وَلَا تَقْرَبُوا which means do not even come close. This teaches us that Allāh ﷻ stopped fornication at the root; those things which will lead a person towards fornication are also forbidden.

Lineage of Mankind

In the next verse of Sūrah Hujurāt, Allāh ﷻ says,

يَا أَيُّهَا النَّاسُ إِنَّا خَلَقْنَاكُم مِّن ذَكَرٍ وَأُنثَى وَجَعَلْنَاكُمْ شُعُوبًا وَقَبَائِلَ لِتَعَارَفُوا إِنَّ أَكْرَمَكُمْ عِندَ اللهِ أَتْقَاكُمْ إِنَّ اللهَ عَلِيمٌ خَبِيرٌ

"O mankind, indeed We have created you from a male and a female and made you into races and tribes so that you may identify one another. Surely the noblest of you in Allāh's sight is the most righteous. Indeed Allāh is All-Knowing, All-Aware." (49:13)

In the previous verse, Allāh ﷻ spoke to the believers regarding the spiritual illnesses. However, in this verse, Allāh ﷻ addresses the whole of mankind.

The word لِتَعَارَفُوْا comes from the word عُرْف which means to be recognised in society. Lineage is not something one should boast about. It is for the sake of identifying one another. In the Aḥādīth it mentions,

$$تُنْكَحُ الْمَرْأَةُ لِأَرْبَعٍ : لِمَالِهَا ، وَلِحَسَبِهَا ، وَلِجَمَالِهَا ، وَلِدِيْنِهَا ، فَاظْفَرْ بِذَاتِ الدِّيْنِ تَرِبَتْ يَدَاكَ$$

"A woman is married for four reasons: her wealth, her beauty, her lineage and her religion, be successful with the one who possesses religion. If you do not, you will regret it." (Bukhārī, Muslim)

Someone once asked Sayyidunā Hasan Ibn Ali ؓ who he should get his daughter married to as she was of marriageable age? Sayyidunā Hasan Ibn Ali ؓ gave a beautiful reply,

$$زَوِّجْهَا مَنْ يَّخَافُ اللهَ ، فَإِنْ أَحَبَّهَا أَكْرَمَهَا ، وَإِنْ أَبْغَضَهَا لَمْ يَظْلِمْهَا$$

"Get her married to a person who fears Allāh ﷻ. If he loves her, he will honour her. If he dislikes her, he will not oppress her."

In the verse, Allāh ﷻ mentions that He made us into tribes in order to identify and recognise one another; not to boast to one other. If everybody was created the same, we would not have been able to recognise each other. We have different ethnicities, for example Pakistāni, Gujarāti, Bangladeshi to recognise each other.

Once, two young boys were boasting to one another about their lineage and during their argument one said, "I am Siddīqi" (from the genealogy of Sayyidunā Abū Bakr Siddīq ﷺ). The other boy said: "I am Fārūqi" (from the genealogy of Sayyidunā Umar ﷺ). A third boy intervened and said, "Why are you both arguing? I am better than both of you; I am Ādami!" (from the genealogy of Sayyidunā Ādam علیہ السلام).

Status of Sayyidunā Bilāl ﷺ

Allāh ﷻ says,

$$ إِنَّ أَكْرَمَكُمْ عِنْدَ اللّٰهِ أَتْقَاكُمْ $$

"Surely the noblest of you in Allāh's sight is the one who is the most righteous." (49:13)

This verse was revealed after the conquest of Makkah Mukarramah. When the time for Adhān was approaching, the Holy Prophet ﷺ instructed Sayyidunā Bilāl ﷺ to go and give the Adhān on the roof of the Ka'bah. A person from the Quraysh saw this and said, "All praise is to Allāh ◉ that my father is not alive to see this day. How could this Negro stand on the roof of the Ka'bah and give the Adhān?" Another person remarked, "Could the Holy Prophet ◉ not find anybody else to give the Adhān?"

Sayyidunā Abū Sufyān ◉, who had newly accepted Islām said, "I am not going to say anything because the Lord of the heavens and the earth will inform the Holy Prophet ◉, therefore it is better for me to stay quiet."

Whilst they were discussing this matter amongst themselves, immediately, Sayyidunā Jibrīl ◉ descended with the verses,

يَا أَيُّهَا النَّاسُ إِنَّا خَلَقْنَاكُمْ مِّنْ ذَكَرٍ وَّأُنْثَى وَجَعَلْنَاكُمْ شُعُوْبًا وَّقَبَآئِلَ لِتَعَارَفُوْا إِنَّ أَكْرَمَكُمْ عِنْدَ اللهِ أَتْقَاكُمْ إِنَّ اللهَ عَلِيْمٌ خَبِيْرٌ

"O mankind, indeed We have created you from a male and a female and made you into races and tribes so that you may identify one another. Surely the noblest of you in Allāh's sight is the most righteous. Indeed Allāh is All-Knowing, All-Aware." (49:13)

The Holy Prophet ◉ called all the Companions ◉ including Sayyidunā Bilāl ◉ and said, "The people are all empty (i.e. have no morals whilst Bilāl is full of morals)."

The Holy Prophet ◉ once said regarding Sayyidunā Bilāl ◉,

سَمِعْتُ دَنَّ نَعْلَيْكَ بَيْنَ يَدَيَّ فِي الْجَنَّةِ

"O Bilāl, whenever I go into Jannah I hear your footsteps in front of me."

Sayyidunā Bilāl ؓ exclaimed, "After performing Istinjā, I perform Wudhu and pray two Rakats of Tahiyyatul Wudhu."
(Bukhāri, Muslim)

Sayyidunā Bilāl ؓ would try and remain in the state of purity. Whenever he performed Wudhu or Ghusl, he would pray optional Salāh, thus this enabled his footsteps to be heard by the Holy Prophet ﷺ in Jannah. When Sayyidunā Bilāl ؓ was about to get married, he went to his future father-in-law with the proposal and said:

أَنَا بِلَالٌ وَهٰذَا أَخِيْ ، كُنَّا عَبْدَيْنِ فَأَعْتَقَنَا اللهُ ، وَكُنَّا ضَالِّيْنَ فَهَدَانَا اللهُ ، فَإِنْ تَنْكِحُوْنَا فَالْحَمْدُ لِلهِ ، وَاِنْ تَمْنَعُوْنَا فَاللهُ اَكْبَرُ

"I am Bilāl and this is my brother. We were both slaves and Allāh ﷻ freed us. We were all astray and Allāh ﷻ guided us. If you accept the marriage proposal then all praise is for Allāh ﷻ. If you do not accept the marriage proposal, then Allāh ﷻ is the greatest (i.e. Allāh ﷻ will provide something else)." (Hayātus Sahābah)

It has been narrated by Imām Bukhāri ؒ in his Sahīh that the Sahābah ؓ asked the Holy Prophet ﷺ, "Who is the most noblest?"

The Holy Prophet ﷺ replied,

$$إِنَّ اَكْرَمَكُمْ عِنْدَ اللهِ اَتْقَاكُمْ$$

"Surely the noblest of you in Allāh's sight, is the one who is the most righteous amongst you." (49:13)

The Sahābah ؓ said, "We are not asking regarding that." The Holy Prophet ﷺ said to the Sahābah ؓ, "If you are thinking about family status, the most noble is Yūsuf because he is the only person who is a Prophet himself, his father, Yā'qūb is a Prophet, his grandfather, Ishāq is a Prophet and his great grandfather, Ibrāhīm is a Prophet too."

$$اَلْكَرِيْمُ ابْنُ الْكَرِيْمِ ابْنِ الْكَرِيْمِ ابْنِ الْكَرِيْمِ يُوْسُفُ بْنُ يَعْقُوْبَ بْنِ إِسْحَاقَ بْنِ إِبْرَاهِيْمَ$$
$$عَلَيْهِمُ السَّلَامُ$$

The Sahābah ؓ said, "We are not asking regarding that." The Holy Prophet ﷺ said to the Sahābah ؓ, "Are you asking with regards to the tribes of the Arabs?

$$خِيَارُكُمْ فِي الْجَاهِلِيَّةِ خِيَارُكُمْ فِي الْإِسْلَامِ إِذَا فَقِهُوْا$$

"The best of you during the days of ignorance is the best of you in the days of Islām with the condition that they have the true understanding of religion."

Possessing true knowledge of the religion is very important. Upon one occasion, Hasan Basri ؓ heard somebody praising a particular

44

scholar. He asked him, "Do you know who a Faqīh is?" When he wanted to know, Hasan Basri ﷦ said,

$$إِنَّمَا الْفَقِيْهُ اَلزَّاهِدُ فِي الدُّنْيَا ، اَلرَّاغِبُ فِي الْآخِرَةِ ، اَلْبَصِيْرُ بِأَمْرِ دِيْنِه ، اَلْمُدَاوِمُ عَلٰى عِبَادَةِ رَبِّه$$

"A Faqīh is one who holds no inclination towards the worldly life, one who has inclination for the Hereafter, one who has knowledge of the matters pertaining to Dīn (religion) and one who is punctual and constant upon the worship of Allāh ﷻ."
(Mirqāt, Volume 1, Page 140)

The Holy Prophet ﷺ has said,

$$إِنَّ اللهَ لَا يَنْظُرُ إِلٰى صُوَرِكُمْ وَأَمْوَالِكُمْ وَلٰكِنْ يَّنْظُرُ إِلٰى قُلُوْبِكُمْ وَأَعْمَالِكُمْ$$

"Indeed Allāh ﷻ does not look at your appearance or wealth but looks at your heart and actions." (Muslim)

Importance of Taqwā

Taqwā comes from the word وِقَايَة, which means a barrier. When a person has the quality of Taqwā within them, it means the person has a barrier in place between himself and those actions which are Harām and Makrūh Tahrīmī. It is also a barrier from omitting obligatory actions, Wājib actions and Sunnah Mu'akkadah actions.

Whenever a person with Taqwā wishes to commit a sin, the fear of Allāh ﷻ comes into the mind, thus, the individual stays away from committing immoral acts. Slandering, backbiting and being suspicious are all Harām acts. Hence, by acquiring Taqwā, a person will be saved from committing these actions.

The Holy Prophet ﷺ has said in one of his beautiful Du'ās,

اَللّٰهُمَّ اقْسِمْ لَنَا مِنْ خَشْيَتِكَ مَاتَحُوْلُ بِهِ بَيْنَنَا وَبَيْنَ مَعَصِيَتِكَ

"O Allāh, bestow us with your fear (that certain amount) which will become a barrier between ourselves and our sins." (Tirmizi)

The word مِنْ in the Arabic language denotes تَبْعِيْض (partiality) i.e. we ask Allāh ﷻ to bestow us with *some* fear (a certain amount), not *all* because if we had the full fear of Allāh ﷻ, we would be unable to eat, drink, sleep etc.

If we want to adopt Taqwā, we need to keep the following verse in mind,

يَا أَيُّهَا الَّذِيْنَ اٰمَنُوا اتَّقُوا اللهَ وَكُوْنُوا مَعَ الصَّادِقِيْنَ

"O you who believe, fear Allāh and remain in the company of the truthful." (9:119)

Allāmah Ālūsi ﷺ commentating on this verse explains how long one should stay in the company of the pious people. He says,

$$\text{خَالِطُوْهُمْ حَتّٰى تَكُوْنُوْا مِثْلَهُمْ}$$

"Be with them until you become like them."

It should not be that one day is spent in the Masjid and the rest of the days a person does not carry it on. For all of these evil habits we possess, we must make an effort to eradicate them. We need to realise the importance of good company and creating strong brotherhood. It is of vital importance that we maintain good thoughts about our Muslim brothers and sisters; this is the foundation. If we start to have doubts, evil thoughts and suspicion about people, then that will ultimately lead to spying and backbiting.

If we can keep this Hadīth in mind,

$$\text{اَلْمُؤْمِنُ مِرْاٰةُ الْمُؤْمِنِ}$$

"A believer is a mirror of a believer." (Tabarāni)

We will always want goodness and happiness for our Muslim brothers and sisters. We will always wish that they are prospering and are in a good state. We need to ask ourselves when was the last time we saw our Muslim brother or sister happy and read the Du'ā expressing our joy and happiness upon their happiness,

أَضْحَكَ اللهُ سِنَّكَ

"May Allāh keep you cheerful" (Bukhāri)

Sayyidunā Abdullāh Ibn Mas'ūd ﷺ was reciting some Du'ās and the Holy Prophet ﷺ was listening and was saying Āmīn upon his Du'ās. Sayyidunā Abū Bakr ﷺ and Sayyidunā Umar ﷺ were both also present. Sayyidunā Umar ﷺ thought he would be the first one to go and give the glad tidings to Sayyidunā Abdullāh Ibn Mas'ūd ﷺ that the Holy Prophet ﷺ had heard him and he was very happy with him. Sayyidunā Umar ﷺ went straight away after they went home. However, Sayyidunā Abdullāh Ibn Mas'ūd ﷺ replied, "Alhamdulillāh, Abū Bakr came before you and has already informed me regarding this."

In terms of giving good news, the Sahābah ﷺ were always eager to inform one another. In these matters we should always compete with each other. We need to try our best to become a mirror for each other.

May Allāh ﷺ give us the ability to act upon what has been said.

وَاٰخِرُ دَعْوَانَا أَنِ الْحَمْدُ لِلّٰهِ رَبِّ الْعَالَمِيْنَ

Part 2

Curing The Diseased Heart

نَحْمَدُهُ وَنُصَلِّيْ عَلَى رَسُوْلِهِ الْكَرِيْمِ

اَمَّا بَعْدُ فَاَعُوْذُ بِاللهِ مِنَ الشَّيْطَانِ الرَّجِيْمِ بِسْمِ اللهِ الرَّحْمٰنِ الرَّحِيْمِ :

قَدْ اَفْلَحَ مَنْ زَكَّاهَا وَقَدْ خَابَ مَنْ دَسَّاهَا

صَدَقَ اللهُ الْعَظِيْمُ

Ability is from Allāh ﷻ

One important point we have to remember and bear in mind, is that Allāh ﷻ chooses the people Himself to come to these kinds of gatherings. Without the Tawfīq from Allāh ﷻ, no-one can go to the Masjid, no-one can come to the Madrasah, no-one can carry out any good deeds without the Tawfīq; without the ability given by Allāh ﷻ.

This reminds me of an incident whereby a master was walking with his servant towards the market place. Whilst proceeding to the market, the Adhān was called. The servant was very punctual and steadfast in his Salāh and vice versa, the master was very neglectful. After the Adhān took place, the servant pleaded to the master and said, ''Please let me go to the Masjid in order to perform my Salāh. I will join you at the market place.'' The servant pleaded a number of times, so in the end, the master gave in and said, "Okay, you go to the Masjid. I will stand outside the Masjid waiting for you, so quickly just read your Fardh and after you complete them, immediately come out of the Masjid."

The servant performed the Salāh with the people and after the Salāh was completed, everybody started to emerge. However, the servant remained inside and continuously read Salāh. He was seated there doing the Munājāt (speaking) to Allāh ﷻ. Due to the servant spending extra time, the master was beginning to get frustrated. He shouted from outside the Masjid,

اے رمضانی تو آتا کیوں نہیں

"O' Ramazāni! What is wrong with you? Why are you not coming out?"

The servant replied back,

وہ مجھے آنے نہیں دیتا

"He is not letting me come out."

Seeing that there was only one person in the Masjid. As there was only one pair of shoes and everybody else had left, the master shouted out in fury,

تجھے کون آنے نہیں دیتا

"Who is not letting you come out?"

The servant gave a very beautiful reply,

وہ جو آپ کو باہر سے اندر آنے دے رہا ہے نہیں دے رہا ہے وہ مجھے اندر سے باہر آنے نہیں
دے رہا ہے

"The one who is not letting you in is not letting me out."

Allāh ﷻ had given the servant the Tawfīq (ability) to go to the Masjid, but the master did not have the Tawfīq hence, he remained outside the Masjid.

In a similar manner, whenever we get this opportunity from Allāh ﷻ where we are able to carry out good deeds, whether it may be coming to the Dhikr Majlis, whether it is going to the Masjid to perform our Salāh in Jamāʾah, whether it is going to listen to a lecture, whether it is going to help a Muslim brother or Muslim sister, we should always express our gratitude to Allāh ﷻ for giving us this opportunity.

One of the main objectives for sitting within this blessed gathering is that we learn about spirituality - curing the diseased heart, which is the topic of today's speech.

Prior to the Qurʾanic verse recited within the sermon, Allāh ﷻ takes seven oaths,

وَالشَّمْسِ وَضُحْهَا وَالْقَمَرِ إِذَا تَلْهَا وَالنَّهَارِ إِذَا جَلْهَا وَالَّيْلِ إِذَا يَغْشُهَا وَالسَّمَاءِ وَمَا بَنْهَا
وَالْأَرْضِ وَمَا طَحْهَا وَنَفْسٍ وَّمَا سَوْهَا

**"I swear by the sun and its brightness, by the moon when it fol-
lows, by the day when it displays its brightness, by the night
when it envelops it, by the sky and the One who constructed it,
by the earth and the One who spread it and by the soul (Nafs)
and the One who perfected it." (91:1-7)**

After taking these seven oaths, Allāh ﷻ says,

قَدْ أَفْلَحَ مَنْ زَكّٰهَا

**"Indeed, the one who has purified his Nafs (i.e. the heart) is the
one who is successful." (91:9)**

Conversely Allāh ﷻ says,

وَقَدْ خَابَ مَنْ دَسّٰهَا

"Indeed, the one who soiled his Nafs will be at loss." (91:10)

Hard-Heartedness

Shāh Walīullāh Muhaddith Dehlawī ﷦ writes in one of his famous works, 'Hujjatullāhil Bāligah' in the chapter of Fitan (trials and tribulations):

$$\text{اِعْلَمْ اَنَّ الْفِتَنَ عَلٰی اَقْسَامٍ}$$

"Know that indeed Fitnah is of many types."

In this chapter, he mentions many different types of Fitan (trials). Firstly he writes,

$$\text{مِنْهَا فِتْنَةُ الرَّجُلِ فِیْ نَفْسِهِ بِاَنْ یَقْسُوَ قَلْبُهُ فَلَا یَجِدُ حَلَاوَةَ الطَّاعَةِ وَ لَا لَذَّةَ الْمُنَاجَاةِ}$$

"There is the trial which is within a person which makes his heart become very hard that he does not achieve or feel the sweetness of obedience to Allāh ﷻ."

He is devoid of the sensation and happiness that one should achieve after carrying out the orders of Allāh ﷻ. The person does not achieve the لَذَّةُ (enjoyment) of اَلْمُنَاجَاةُ (one to one supplication with Allāh ﷻ).

This is truly a devastating Fitnah! We are sadly the living statistics of this Fitnah. We do not wish to attend the Masjid, we do not possess the zeal to recite the Holy Qur'ān and we do not want to attend an

Islamic gathering—this is extremely dangerous!

The Qur'anic verse states,

وَمَنْ أَعْرَضَ عَنْ ذِكْرِيْ فَإِنَّ لَهُ مَعِيْشَةً ضَنْكًا وَّنَحْشُرُهٗ يَوْمَ الْقِيٰمَةِ أَعْمٰى

"The person who ignores My remembrance (without any valid reason) will have a constrained life (he will go through a hard life in this world and in the hereafter) and We will gather him on the Day of Judgement blind." (20:124)

The word 'Dhikr' here could refer to attending the Masjid or coming to gatherings i.e. coming to congregate for those things which are categorised as the obedience of Allāh ﷻ.

Allāh ﷻ mentions in Sūrah Baqarah regarding three types of stones,

وَإِنَّ مِنَ الْحِجَارَةِ لَمَا يَتَفَجَّرُ مِنْهُ الْأَنْهَارُ وَإِنَّ مِنْهَا لَمَا يَشَّقَّقُ فَيَخْرُجُ مِنْهُ الْمَاءُ وَإِنَّ مِنْهَا لَمَا يَهْبِطُ مِنْ خَشْيَةِ اللهِ

1. There are those types of stones when water gushes forth, it make streams, canals, rivers and oceans.

2. There are those stones, that when it splits, water trickles.

3. There are those stones from which water does not flow out but due to the fear of Allāh ﷻ, it rolls.

Allāh ﷺ is saying, "O human beings! you do not even fall into any of these categories; your hearts have become even more harder than the stones!

A Companion ﷺ states that once they were sitting in the company of the Holy Prophet ﷺ and he mentioned regarding Jannah and Jahannam. Many Sahābah ﷺ started to cry but he could not bring himself to cry. He therefore went to the Holy Prophet ﷺ complaining regarding his hard heartedness, how could he cure this diseased heart? The Holy Prophet ﷺ replied in a beautiful manner:

جُمُوْدُ الْعَيْنِ مِنْ قَسْوَةِ الْقَلْبِ وَقَسْوَةُ الْقَلْبِ مِنْ كَثْرَةِ الذُّنُوْبِ وَكَثْرَةُ الذُّنُوْبِ مِنْ نِسْيَانِ
الْمَوْتِ وَ نِسْيَانُ الْمَوْتِ مِنْ طُوْلِ الْأَمَلِ وَطُوْلُ الْأَمَلِ مِنْ شِدَّةِ الْحِرْصِ وَ شِدَّةُ الْحِرْصِ مِنْ
حُبِّ الدُّنْيَا وَ حُبُّ الدُّنْيَا رَأْسُ كُلِّ خَطِيْئَةٍ

"The lack of tears is due to hard heartedness and hard heartedness is because of excessive sinning. Excessive sinning is due to forgetting death and forgetting death is due to lengthy desires. Lengthy desires is because of extreme greed and extreme greed is due to love of the world. The love of the world is the root of all evil."
(Minhājus Sunnah)

Stages of Sinning

Imām Tirmizi ﷺ mentions in his Sunan,

إِذَا أَذْنَبَ الْعَبْدُ ذَنْبًا فَكَانَتْ نُكْتَةٌ سَوْدَاءُ فِي قَلْبِهِ فَإِنْ زَادَ زَادَتْ

"When a servant of Allāh ﷻ commits a sin, a black spot falls on the heart. If the servant continues to commit sins, these black spots continue to increase."

فَإِنْ تَابَ صُقِلَتْ قَلْبُهُ فَذٰلِكَ قَوْلُهُ تَعَالٰى

If the servant does Tawbah and repents sincerely, the heart becomes polished. However, if the servant continues to sin, then Allāh ﷻ has mentioned,

كَلَّا بَلْ رَانَ عَلٰى قُلُوبِهِمْ مَّا كَانُوْا يَكْسِبُوْنَ

"Nay! But that which they used to commit has covered their hearts with rust." (83:14)

Allāh ﷻ mentions the next stage,

خَتَمَ اللهُ عَلٰى قُلُوبِهِمْ وَعَلٰى سَمْعِهِمْ وَعَلٰى أَبْصَارِهِمْ غِشَاوَةٌ وَلَهُمْ عَذَابٌ عَظِيْمٌ

"Allāh has set a seal on their hearts and on their hearing; and on their eyes there is a covering and for them awaits a mighty punishment." (2:7)

The heart becomes totally sealed. The eyes, ears, every organ is stamped and sealed. The next stage is,

صُمٌّ بُكُمٌ عُمْيٌ فَهُمْ لَا يَرْجِعُونَ

"Deaf, dumb and blind, they shall not return." (2:18)

The person becomes spiritually deaf, dumb and blind despite physically being well.

فَإِنَّهَا لَا تَعْمَى الْأَبْصَارُ وَلَكِنْ تَعْمَى الْقُلُوبُ الَّتِي فِي الصُّدُورِ

"For indeed it is not the eyes that turn blind, but what turns blind is the hearts contained in the chests." (22:46)

He has got the eyesight but not the insight. He has the بَصَارَتْ (Basārat—eyesight) but not the بَصِيْرَتْ (Basīrat—insight).

In one Qur'anic verse Allāh ﷻ says,

يُعَذِّبُ مَنْ يَّشَاءُ وَيَرْحَمُ مَنْ يَّشَاءُ وَإِلَيْهِ تُقْلَبُونَ

"Allāh punishes whom He wills and has mercy on whom He wills and to Him you are to be returned." (29:21)

Some of the Mufassirūn (scholars of Qur'ān exegesis) mention that يُعَذِّبُ مَنْ يَّشَاءُ refers to يُعَذِّبُ بِالْحِرْصِ (Allāh ﷻ punishes the person with greed) and that وَيَرْحَمُ مَنْ يَّشَاءُ refers to وَيَرْحَمُ بِالْقَنَاعَةِ (Allāh ﷻ shows mercy through giving the person contentment of the heart.)

Even whilst living in this world, a person may be going through so many different kinds of trials and tribulations because one has not purified the heart; a person always wants more. Whenever we want to do something we have to reflect, contemplate and ponder, why are we doing this thing?

Four Objectives

Hakīmul Ummah, Shaykh Ashraf Ali Thānwi ﷫ gives the example of a house. He mentions that we all purchase houses. We either have our own homes or we rent a house etc. However, when purchasing a house, what are the Maqāsid (objectives)?

There are four مَقْصَدُ (objectives) and this is not only restricted to a house; it can apply to many fields.

1.   Firstly, when a person wishes to purchase a house, the main objective they have is - رهَائْش - accommodation.

The person wants to purchase a house in order to live. Accommodation could even be in a hut or in a tent, so at least it will safeguard the person from the rain and wind and will safeguard the person from the heat of the sun. We see millions of people, including our own

59

Muslim brothers and sisters, living around the world who do not even have tents; they do not even have any shelter over themselves. So رهائش (accommodation) is the minimum requirement.

2.   Secondly, the objective is اسائش - comfort; to make things easy for the person.

For example, an individual has a hut or tent but he is thinking to himself that the rain is still coming inside due to the tent or hut not being strong enough; it is not waterproof or there are still many problems occurring within this house. So the person builds the hut or the house with proper bricks, concrete and cement. This is perfectly fine.

3.   The third objective is آرائش - beautification. The person has got a house, hut or building made of bricks, cement etc. However, there is no paint, wallpaper, carpets or curtains, so the person beautifies the house. There is no problem with this also.

With all these three objectives, there is no problem. The problem lies with the fourth objective.

4.   The fourth objective is نمائش - to display beauty in order to compete with other people i.e. to show off in front of people or to exhibit that one is superior over the other. This is impermis-

sible.

When guests come to visit the individual's house, they do not only say it is beautiful, rather the person himself is thinking that his house is standing out in front of all the other houses.

Hakīmul Ummah, Shaykh Ashraf Ali Thānwi ﷺ uses an example of a house. However, these categories can apply to anything. If a person wishes to purchase some clothes, food etc. then one should always keep these four objectives in mind.

Regarding showing off, the Holy Prophet ﷺ has said,

مَنْ صَلّٰى يُرَائِيْ فَقَدْ أَشْرَكَ ، وَمَنْ صَامَ يُرَائِيْ فَقَدْ أَشْرَكَ ، وَمَنْ تَصَدَّقَ يُرَائِيْ فَقَدْ أَشْرَكَ

"A person who has performed prayers with ostentation has ascribe partners to Allāh ﷻ. A person who has fasted with ostentation has ascribed partners to Allāh ﷻ. A person who gave in charity with os-tentation has ascribed partners to Allāh ﷻ."
(Musnad Ahmad)

<u>Definition of Pride</u>

One main illness which is prevalent and is the root of all illnesses is pride and arrogance. When a person has pride present within himself, this will cause him to have so many other illnesses. If we want to cure our hearts, then we need to take that pride and arrogance away from our hearts.

The Holy Prophet ﷺ has said in a Hadīth which has been narrated by Imām Muslim ﷺ in his Sahīh,

لَا يَدْخُلُ الْجَنَّةَ مَنْ كَانَ فِي قَلْبِه مِثْقَالُ ذَرَّةٍ مِّنْ كِبْرٍ، قَالَ رَجُلٌ: إِنَّ الرَّجُلَ يُحِبُّ أَنْ يَكُوْنَ
ثَوْبُه حَسَنًا، وَنَعْلُه حَسَنَةً، قَالَ: إِنَّ اللهَ جَمِيْلٌ يُحِبُّ الْجَمَالَ

"That person will not enter Paradise who has a mustard amount of pride within himself." A Sahabi ﷺ then asked, "Indeed a person likes that his clothes are clean and pleasing and he likes that his shoes are good (is that permissible?)" The Holy Prophet ﷺ replied, "Indeed Allāh ﷻ is beautiful, He likes beauty (there is no problem with that)."

The Holy Prophet ﷺ has further explained what pride is in the Hadīth,

اَلْكِبْرُ بَطَرُ الْحَقِّ وَغَمْطُ النَّاسِ
"Pride is to reject the truth and belittle people." (Muslim)

There are two aspects mentioned. The first is بَطَرُ الْحَقّ one denies and rejects the truth. A person may tell his Muslim brother to keep a beard and the brother replies, "Who are you to tell me?!" A person may say, "Brother, you should keep your trousers above your ankles because the Hadīth says,

مَا أَسْفَلَ مِنَ الْكَعْبَيْنِ مِنَ الْإِزَارِ فَفِي النَّارِ

"That part of one's clothes which is below the ankles will burn in the fire of Jahannam." (Bukhāri)

The brother responds rudely, "Who are you to tell me! I do not do it with the intention of Takabbur (pride)!" So this is بَطَرُ الْحَقّ which is a sign of pride. Many people say, "Even if the biggest scholar was to come and tell me that this is Harām, I will still not refrain." This is a sign of the highest level of pride and arrogance.

The second aspect of pride غَمْطُ النَّاس - one belittles people. The Holy Prophet ﷺ did not say وَغَمْطُ الْمُسْلِمِ (belittling a Muslim). The Holy Prophet ﷺ said غَمْطُ النَّاس (belittles people) so even to belittle a non-Muslim is not permissible as well.

Pride and Vanity

There are two words in the Arabic language:

1. تَكَبُّر - Pride
2. عُجُب - Vanity

تَكَبُّر(pride) is when a person thinks they are superior and they also think the opponent to be lower than them. عُجُب (vanity) is when the individual thinks oneself to be superior, however the individual does not think the other person is lower than him - both are not permissible.

The Qur'ān mentions regarding the Battle of Hunayn. Allāh ﷻ says,

لَقَدْ نَصَرَكُمُ اللّٰهُ فِىْ مَوَاطِنَ كَثِيْرَةٍ وَّيَوْمَ حُنَيْنٍ إِذْ أَعْجَبَتْكُمْ كَثْرَتُكُمْ فَلَمْ تُغْنِ عَنْكُمْ شَيْئًا وَّضَاقَتْ عَلَيْكُمُ الْأَرْضُ بِمَا رَحُبَتْ ثُمَّ وَلَّيْتُمْ مُّدْبِرِيْنَ

"Allāh has helped you in many regions and (even) on the day of Hunayn, when your great number pleased you, but it did not avail you at all, and the earth was confining for you despite its vastness, then you turned back fleeing. (9:25)

During the beginning of the Battle of Hunayn, whilst the Sahābah ﷺ were confronting the enemies, a thought came within their minds that as the enemies are less in number i.e. 4,000, they (i.e. the Sahābah ﷺ) will win because their army is bigger in number being 12,000.

Previously, in all the battles which the Sahābah ﷺ had fought, they were always less in number. During the Battle of Badr, there were 313 ill-equipped Muslims compared to 1,000 well-equipped non-Muslims. In the battle of Uhud, there were 1,000 Muslims and 3,000 non-Muslims. In the battle of the Trench, there were only 1,500 Muslims and there were over 10,000 non Muslims. Therefore, this was the first battle in which the Muslims were higher in number, hence, this thought came within their minds that they are undefeatable.

Despite having a large army, Allāh ﷻ says: "فَلَمْ تُغْنِ عَنْكُمْ شَيْئًا This did not help you at all." The tribe of Ghitfān started to shoot arrows towards the Sahābah ﷺ who started to lose ground. Thus, the Holy Prophet ﷺ himself went forward into the midst of the battlefield and said,

$$أَنَا النَّبِيُّ لَا كَذِبْ أَنَا ابْنُ عَبْدِ الْمُطَّلِبْ$$

"I am the Prophet; I am not a liar. I am the grandson of Abdul Muttalib." (Bukhāri)

Through the supplication of the Holy Prophet ﷺ and the Sahābah ﷺ, Allāh ﷻ sent His Divine tranquillity and peace and the Muslims won the battle,

$$ثُمَّ أَنْزَلَ اللهُ سَكِينَتَهُ عَلَى رَسُولِهِ وَعَلَى الْمُؤْمِنِينَ وَأَنْزَلَ جُنُودًا لَّمْ تَرَوْهَا$$

"Then Allāh sent down His tranquillity upon His Messenger and upon the believers and sent down soldiers (i.e. angels) whom you did not see." (9:26)

The Sahābah ﷺ were the best of all people in the presence of the best of all humanity; the Holy Prophet ﷺ. However, due to the spiritual malady of عُجْب entering into their hearts, Allāh ﷻ reprimanded them. Every person needs to think that Allāh ﷻ alone is the Helper and He alone is the One Who can assist.

Eradicating Pride

Hakīmul Ummah, Shaykh Ashraf Ali Thānwi ﷺ says, "I always think myself lower than all the Muslims. I am much more lower in status than all the Muslims at present and in the future, I am even lower than the disbelievers. Why? It is possible that these disbelievers accept Imān and they become believers and better than me." If a person can always keep this in mind that I am the lowest of the low, then this pride and arrogance will eventually go.

Upon one occasion, somebody announced in the Masjid, "Let the worst person who is seated within this Masjid come quickly outside (i.e. at the entrance)." Immediately, Junaid Baghdādi ﷺ was the first one to rush out and in reality, he was the most pious.

When Allāmah Sayyid Sulaimān Nadwi ﷺ went to meet Shaykh

Thānwi 🕮 in order to take Bai'ah (spiritual allegiance), Shaykh Thānwi 🕮 asked, "A scholar of your calibre! You want to take Bai'ah to me?!" The reason Shaykh Thānwi 🕮 said this is because Allāmah Sayyid Sulaimān Nadwi 🕮 was from Nadwa and the Ulamā of Nadwa regarded themselves to be much more superior than the Ulamā of Deoband in terms of knowledge. Therefore, for him to come over was something strange and amazing. Once the news reached the people of Nadwa, that Allāmah Sayyid Sulaiman Nadwi 🕮 had gone to Thāna Bhāwan, they were extremely sad to this extent that the next day they edited the newspaper in black, expressing their grief upon the incident.

What is Tasawwuf?

When Allāmah Sayyid Sulaimān Nadwi 🕮 visited Shaykh Thānwi 🕮, he asked him regarding Tasawwuf (spiritual development). Shaykh Thānwi 🕮 replied, "A great scholar of your calibre is asking a student like me?!"

Subhān-Allāh, the تَوَاضُع (humility) and اِخْلَاص (sincerity) these people had is truly astounding! Shaykh Thānwi 🕮 replied, "I will tell you what my teachers have taught me: Tasawwuf (spiritual development) is when a person thinks to himself that he is nothing when he is everything and when he starts to think to himself that he is something then he is nothing."

Shaykh Thānwi ﷺ once said a thought provoking statement:

بزرگی کو طلب کرنا فرض عین ہے ، اپنے آپ کو بزرگ سمجھنا حرام ہے

"To seek to achieve piety is Fardh (compulsory) and to perceive that
you are pious is Harām (forbidden)."

To try and achieve piety is Fardh; this is the reason why we have
come here today - in order to try and achieve it. However, to perceive and think to yourself that you are pious is Harām. Subhān-
Allāh!

Allāh ﷻ says,

فَلَا تُزَكُّوٓا أَنفُسَكُمْ ۖ هُوَ أَعْلَمُ بِمَنِ ٱتَّقَىٰٓ

**"Do not ascribe purity to yourselves. He (Allāh) is most knowl-
edgeable regarding who is pious."(53:32)**

After graduating from Dārul Ulūm Deoband, Maulānā Muhammadullāh ﷺ, famously known as Hāfiz Huzūr ﷺ, went to meet
Shaykh Thānwi ﷺ. The reason why he went was to purify his Nafs
and to cure the diseases of the Nafs.

After introducing himself (i.e. after explaining that he wanted to purify himself), Shaykh Thānwi ﷺ looked at his face and said, "You
have got pride in yourself." These were the Hakīms (physicians) of
this Ummah! Vice versa, these were the true Murīds (seekers of spir-

ituality). Maulānā Muhammadullāh ﷺ said, "Shaykh! that is the reason why I have come here." Shaykh Thānwi ﷺ hence gave the spiritual prescription:

1. Firstly, you are required to straighten and sort out the shoes of
    the people who come into the Masjid - they will leave their
    shoes everywhere. Your job is to straighten their shoes and
    place them on the shoe racks.

2. Secondly, after every Salāh, you must stand and make an an-
    nouncement, "O worshippers! Please do Du'ā for me because I
    have got pride in myself."

In our time, if a Shaykh instructed us to do this, we would say that
this is it, my Bai'ah with you is finished! These people, on the other
hand, were the true servants and seekers; they possessed such deep
concern pertaining to curing the diseased heart.

Maulānā Muhammadullāh ﷺ continued this prescription for two
weeks. After two weeks, he went back to meet Shaykh Thānwi ﷺ.
Shaykh Thānwi ﷺ said to him that half of the pride was gone and
there was still the other half left. So Maulānā Muhammadullāh ﷺ
continued for another few weeks. After that, he went back to Shaykh
Thānwi ﷺ and Shaykh Thānwi ﷺ said to him, "Alhamdulillāh, this
illness of yours is gone." Unfortunately, this grave illness is the last
thing that goes from a person because everyone wants to think to

themselves that they are something .

Subhān-Allāh! When I travelled to Thāna Bhāwan, during my recent trip to India, I looked inside the Khānqah. It was truly amazing! In the Khānqah there were very small rooms and the space was enough for just one person; if one was to sleep, one would not be able to move around too much. The person who was showing us around said that these were the rooms where the grand Mufti, Mufti Āzam (Mufti Shafī Sāhib ﷺ) stayed, where Qāri Muhammad Tayyib Sāhib ﷺ stayed, where Maulānā Masīhullāh Khān Sāhib ﷺ stayed and where Allāmah Sayyid Sulaiman Nadwi ﷺ stayed.

All these profound scholars had their own small Hujras (small chambers). They were given all their Ma'mūlāt (daily acts of worship) and all the spiritual remedies and spiritual prescriptions to follow. Eventually, when they came out, one after the other, they actually managed to eradicate all these illnesses from themselves and returned to their homelands guiding the whole nation; each scholar guiding millions of people. Hakīmul Ummah, Shaykh Ashraf Ali Thānwi ﷺ says, "If two scholars come to me, one being spiritually cleansed whilst the other one is not, immediately I will know by just looking at them."

Shaykh Thānwi ﷺ says, "To do your Islāh is Fardh Ayn; not Fardh Kifāyah." This means that if some people do it and others do not do it, it will not be acceptable. We all have to get rid of these spiritual illnesses.

Harms of Pride

The Hadīth mentions,

لَا يَدْخُلُ الْجَنَّةَ مَنْ كَانَ فِي قَلْبِه مِثْقَالُ ذَرَّةٍ مِّنْ كِبْرٍ

"He will not enter Paradise who has got a mustard amount of pride
inside him." (Muslim)

That is why Allāh ﷻ says,

إِنَّهُ لَا يُحِبُّ الْمُسْتَكْبِرِينَ

"Allāh does not love those people who have pride." (16:23)

The word اِسْتِكْبَارُ in Arabic gives the meaning of pretence. So it
refers to those people who pretend i.e. they do not have anything to
show off in reality and do not have any greatness within themselves
but instead they pretend.

In this verse, لَا يُحِبُّ is فعل مضارع (present and future tenses) which
means that Allāh ﷻ does not love them now in the present time and
neither will He love them in the future until this pride is not re-
moved.

وَلَهُ الْكِبْرِيَآءُ فِي السَّمٰوٰتِ وَالْأَرْضِ

"To Allāh alone belongs the grandeur within the heavens and the earth." (45:37)

In this verse, لَهُ gives the meaning of تَخْصِيص. A famous rule within the Arabic language is:

اَلتَّقْدِيمُ مَا حَقُّهُ التَّأْخِيرُ يُفِيْدُ الْحَصَرَ

Something which is supposed to come afterwards but instead comes before in the sentence, gives the meaning of exclusiveness. In this verse it means that highness is solely for Allāh ﷻ and not any body else.

A Hadīth Qudsī narrated by Imām Abū Dāwūd ﷺ and Imām Ibn Mājah ﷺ mentions that Allāh ﷻ says,

اَلْكِبْرِيَاءُ رِدَائِي، وَالْعَظَمَةُ إِزَارِي فَمَنْ نَازَعَنِي وَاحِدًا مِّنْهُمَا قَذَفْتُهُ فِي النَّارِ

"Highness is My upper garment and majesty is My lower garment. Whomsoever wants to take any of these garments away frome Me, I will throw him into the fire of Jahannam."

Allāh ﷻ says in Sūrah Baqarah,

وَإِذْ قُلْنَا لِلْمَلَائِكَةِ اسْجُدُوا لِآدَمَ إِلَّا إِبْلِيسَ أَبَى وَاسْتَكْبَرَ وَكَانَ مِنَ الْكَافِرِينَ

"And when We said to the angels (Iblīs was also addressed), "Prostrate yourselves before Ādam." So they all prostrated

72

themselves except Iblīs. He rejected and showed arrogance thus (due to showing arrogance) he immediately became from the disbelievers." (2:34)

It is therefore extremely important and essential that we remove this pride from ourselves!

Virtues of Humility

Sayyidunā Abū Dharr ﷺ possessed the quality of humility to the highest degree which is what Allāh ﷻ loves and wants from His servants.

On one occasion, Sayyidunā Abū Dharr ﷺ was walking towards the Holy Prophet ﷺ. The Holy Prophet ﷺ was with Sayyidunā Jibrīl عليه السلام. Sayyidunā Jibrīl عليه السلام said to the Holy Prophet ﷺ,

هٰذَا اَبُوْ ذَرٍّ قَدْ اَقْبَلَ عَلَيْنَا

"It is Abū Dharr who is coming towards you."

Surprised, the Holy Prophet ﷺ said to Sayyidunā Jibrīl عليه السلام,

اَوَتَعْرِفُوْنَه

"Do you recognise him?!"

Sayyidunā Jibrīl عليه السلام replied,

73

هُوَ اَشْهَرُ عِنْدَنَا مِنْهُ عِنْدَكُمْ

"He is more famous amongst us (the angels) than he is amongst yourselves."

The Holy Prophet ﷺ was very surprised and amazed and asked Sayyidunā Jibrīl عليه السلام,

بِمَاذَا نَالَ هٰذِهِ الْفَضِيْلَةَ

"How did he achieve this virtue?"

Sayyidunā Jibrīl عليه السلام gave two reasons:

1. "لِصِغَرِهٖ فِيْ نَفْسِهٖ - Due to belittling himself." Sayyidunā Abū Dharr ﷺ would always think low of himself.

2. "وَكَثْرَةُ قِرَائَتِهٖ قُلْ هُوَ اللهُ اَحَدٌ - Due to his excessive recitation of Sūrah Ikhlās."

In this day and age, we aspire to be famous on Facebook, Twitter and all the different social media platforms. However, these people were famous amongst the angels!

When Sayyidunā Yūnus عليه السلام was within the stomach of the fish doing the Tasbīh of Allāh ﷻ, proclaiming,

$$\text{لَا إِلٰهَ إِلَّا أَنْتَ سُبْحَانَكَ إِنِّي كُنْتُ مِنَ الظَّالِمِينَ}$$

"There is no deity except You, exalted are You; indeed I am among the wrongdoers" (21:87)

The angels were saying,

$$\text{صَوْتٌ مَعْرُوفٌ مِنْ بِلَادٍ غَرِيبَةٍ}$$

"This is a very famous voice but it is from an unknown place."

They recognised Sayyidunā Yūnus's ﷺ voice because he would engage himself in the worship of Allāh ﷻ and he would engage himself in reciting Tasbīḥāt (glorification). Therefore the angles were very familiar with his voice. Allāh ﷻ said he is within the stomach of the fish. Hence, the angels pleaded for his deliverance as well.

The vital point here is that these people possessed the one to one connection with Allāh ﷻ and this is what we should all aspire to gain.

The Holy Prophet ﷺ mentioned,

$$\text{مَنْ تَوَاضَعَ لِلّٰهِ رَفَعَهُ اللّٰهُ ، فَهُوَ فِي نَفْسِهِ صَغِيرٌ ، وَفِي أَعْيُنِ النَّاسِ عَظِيمٌ ، وَمَنْ تَكَبَّرَ وَضَعَهُ}$$
$$\text{اللّٰهُ عَزَّ وَجَلَّ ، فَهُوَ فِي أَعْيُنِ النَّاسِ صَغِيرٌ ، وَفِي نَفْسِهِ كَبِيرٌ ، وَحَتَّى لَهُوَ أَهْوَنُ عَلَيْهِمْ مِنْ كَلْبٍ}$$
$$\text{أَوْ خِنْزِيرٍ}$$

"The person who humbles himself for the sake of Allāh ﷻ , Allāh ﷻ will raise him. He himself thinks he is very low but in the eyes of

people, (Allāh ﷻ raises his rank to such an extent) the person is amazing and magnificent. On the contrary, a person who shows arrogance (Allāh ﷻ will disgrace that person and as a result) will be disgraceful within the eyes of the people, however, the person himself thinks he is very good. In the eyes of the people the individual becomes so disgraced that he is worse than a dog or a swine.
(Baihaqī in Shua'bul Imān)

Nonetheless, because of pride and arrogance, the individual becomes self-conceited to such an extent that they do not even realise what they are doing.

Mutarrif ﷺ once saw a youngster named Yazīd Ibn Muhallab. Yazīd was walking in a very haughty manner with his chest protruding out and stamping his feet on the ground. Mutarrif ﷺ said to him, "O' my son. You should not walk like this." Yazīd retorted back, "Do you know who I am?!" Mutarrif ﷺ said, "Indeed, I know who you are:

أَوَّلُكَ نُطْفَةٌ قَذِرَةٌ، وَآخِرُكَ جِيْفَةٌ مَذِرَةٌ، وَأَنْتَ بَيْنَ ذٰلِكَ حَامِلُ عَذِرَةٍ

"Your beginning was that you were an impure semen. Your ending is that you are a decomposed dead body and in between you are carrying waste in your body."

Allāh ﷻ says,

قُتِلَ الْإِنْسَٰنُ مَآ أَكْفَرَهُ مِنْ أَيِّ شَيْءٍ خَلَقَهُ مِنْ نُطْفَةٍ

"Let man be destroyed, how ungrateful he is. Does man not real-

**ise what thing Allāh created him from. From that impure se-
men." (80:17-19)**

It is so impure and unclean that if it comes out from the body, one
has to have a Fardh bath. If it touches a person's clothes or body, the
person has to wash his clothes or body.

$$\text{هَلْ أَتَى عَلَى الْإِنْسَانِ حِينٌ مِّنَ الدَّهْرِ لَمْ يَكُنْ شَيْئًا مَّذْكُورًا}$$

**"Hasn't a period of time come upon man when he was not even
worth mentioning." (76:1)**

$$\text{وَاللهُ أَخْرَجَكُم مِّنْ بُطُونِ أُمَّهَاتِكُمْ لَا تَعْلَمُونَ شَيْئًا وَجَعَلَ لَكُمُ السَّمْعَ وَالْأَبْصَارَ وَالْأَفْئِدَةَ}$$
$$\text{لَعَلَّكُمْ تَشْكُرُونَ}$$

**"Allāh has taken you out of the wombs of your mothers when
you had no understanding. He made for you the faculties of listening, seeing and understanding so that you may be grate-
ful." (16:78)**

The illnesses that we have, we need to work on them. If we can ponder and reflect over the words of Mutarrif 🌸 and of Shaykh Thānwi
🌸, we should find these illnesses slowly leaving our hearts.

The Holy Prophet ﷺ made the following Du'ā for acquiring purification of the heart,

$$\text{اَللّٰهُمَّ طَهِّرْ قَلْبِيْ مِنَ النِّفَاقِ وَعَمَلِيْ مِنَ الرِّيَاءِ وَلِسَانِيْ مِنَ الْكَذِبِ وَعَيْنِيْ مِنَ الْخِيَانَةِ،}$$

$$\text{فَإِنَّكَ تَعْلَمُ خَائِنَةَ الْأَعْيُنِ وَمَا تُخْفِي الصُّدُوْرُ}$$

"O Allāh, purify my heart from hypocrisy, my deeds from ostentation, my tongue from lies and my eyes from treachery. Surely You know the treachery of the eyes and what the chests conceal." (Da'wātul Kabīr)

Curing Spiritual Illnesses

Our pious predecessors have mentioned that if a person thinks that he is better than somebody i.e. possesses the evil quality of pride, then the following remedies and measures should be adopted in order to eradicate the illness:

- Firstly, the individual needs to ponder and reflect over the fact that Allāh ﷻ has divinely given them this quality through His infinite mercy despite them not being worthy of it.

- Secondly, Allāh ﷻ has given them this quality but they are not sure if this quality is going to be permanent; Allāh ﷻ can take this away from them at anytime.

- Thirdly, the person whom they think is lower than them may apparently not have the quality which they have, but he may possess a quality which Allāh ﷻ loves better than theirs, hence he may be better than them in the eyes of Allāh ﷻ.

- Fourthly, if the individual who they think is lower than them does not have visible qualities, then it is possible that Allāh ﷻ bestows the person with a quality which will be better than theirs.

- Lastly, if none of the above work, then one should have sympathy for those who may be apparently lower than oneself.

A person should not have pride and arrogance towards a weaker and disadvantaged individual. Subhān-Allāh! The manner in which the pious predecessors actually diagnosed these illnesses and simultaneously, gave remedies is truly remarkable.

Evil Nature of Mocking

Allāh ﷻ devotes one chapter of the Holy Qur'ān to Sayyidunā Luqmān عليه السلام and says,

وَلَقَدْ اٰتَيْنَا لُقْمَانَ الْحِكْمَةَ

"We gave Luqmān wisdom." (31:12)

Due to Sayyidunā Luqmān عليه السلام being black in complexion, short and having big lips, a person once mocked at him and said,

مَا اَقْبَحَ هٰذَا الْوَجْهَ

"How ugly is your face?"

How derogatory the statement was and how angered we would have become if it was said to us. However, a beautiful and thought provoking reply was given by Sayyidunā Luqmān رَضِيَ اللهُ عَنهُ,

اَتَعِيْبُ بِهٰذَا عَلَى النَّقْشِ اَوْ عَلَى النَّقَّاشِ

"Are you finding a fault at the pattern or the pattern maker, the fashion or the fashion maker, the design or the designer."

If a person thinks deeply in that way, they would never ever look down on anybody because if we are pointing a finger at somebody, we are actually in reality, finding a fault in Allāh's ﷻ creation. For any individual who has got a disability - whether it is a mental disability or a physical disability, it is all from Allāh ﷻ. In addition, when we mock at somebody, in reality we are mocking at Allāh ﷻ Who is the Creator.

Next time we make any derogatory comments, we should think deeply. In reality, by making disparaging comments about someone, we are making negative comments towards Allāh ﷻ because it is Allāh ﷻ Who has given a person their appearance.
The Holy Prophet ﷺ has said,

اِنَّكَ لَسْتَ بِخَيْرٍ مِّنْ اَحْمَرَ وَلَا اَسْوَدَ اِلَّا اَنْ تَفْضُلَه بِتَقْوٰى

80

"You are not upon any goodness due to being red-skinned or black-skinned unless you give that virtue with Taqwā (God consciousness)." (Musnad Ahmad)

يَا أَيُّهَا الْإِنْسَانُ مَا غَرَّكَ بِرَبِّكَ الْكَرِيمِ الَّذِي خَلَقَكَ فَسَوَّاكَ فَعَدَلَكَ فِي أَيِّ صُورَةٍ مَا شَاءَ رَكَّبَكَ

"O mankind, what has deceived you from your Merciful Lord Who has created you. He put all the body parts symmetrical; everything is proportionate. He composed you in whichever form He willed. (82:6-8)

Allāh ﷻ composed mankind in such a beautiful appearance that no two people are similar; every single human being is unique.

لَقَدْ خَلَقْنَا الْإِنْسَانَ فِي أَحْسَنِ تَقْوِيمٍ

"Indeed, We have created mankind in the best of form (structure)." (95:4)

وَلَقَدْ كَرَّمْنَا بَنِي آدَمَ وَحَمَلْنَاهُمْ فِي الْبَرِّ وَالْبَحْرِ وَرَزَقْنَاهُم مِّنَ الطَّيِّبَاتِ وَفَضَّلْنَاهُمْ عَلَى كَثِيرٍ مِّمَّنْ خَلَقْنَا تَفْضِيلًا

"We have certainly given dignity and honour to the children of Ādam and We have made them travel on the land and sea and We have provided them from the good things and We have given them (i.e. the children of Ādam) preference over many of Our creation." (17:70)

Mocking people either verbally or by gesturing is Harām. Once by a gesture of the hand, Sayyidah Ā'ishah ﷺ indicated to the Holy Prophet ﷺ that Sayyidah Safiyyah ﷺ the other wife of the Holy Prophet ﷺ, was short. The Holy Prophet ﷺ became very angry and said, "O' Ā'ishah, if that gesture was put into the ocean, it would pollute the ocean." (Abū Dawūd)

Despite Sayyidah Ā'ishah ﷺ being the most beloved to the Holy Prophet ﷺ, he was quick to reprimand her and did not overlook . Rather, when the need arose to reprimand somebody, the Holy Prophet ﷺ always went forward and made sure the matter was sorted out and corrected.

Allāh ﷺ says about the disbelievers,

وَإِذَا مَرُّوا بِهِمْ يَتَغَامَزُوْنَ وَإِذَا انْقَلَبُوْا إِلَى أَهْلِهِمُ انْقَلَبُوْا فَكِهِيْنَ وَإِذَا رَأَوْهُمْ قَالُوْا إِنَّ هَؤُلَاءِ لَضَالُّوْنَ وَمَا أُرْسِلُوْا عَلَيْهِمْ حَافِظِيْنَ

"When the disbelievers pass by the believers they would wink at one another. When they returned to their family, they went enjoying their mockery. And when they saw them, they would say, 'Surely, these are the ones who have gone astray'. Yet they were never sent as guardians over them." (83:30-33)

The ultimate result on the Day of Judgement will be,

فَالْيَوْمَ الَّذِيْنَ اٰمَنُوْا مِنَ الْكُفَّارِ يَضْحَكُوْنَ

"Today, those who believed will laugh at the disbelievers." (83:34)

Sayyidunā Nūh ﷺ said in reply to his nation's sarcastic remarks,

اِنْ تَسْخَرُوْا مِنَّا فَإِنَّا نَسْخَرُ مِنْكُمْ كَمَا تَسْخَرُوْنَ

"If you are mocking at us (then ultimately on the Day of Judgement) we will be mocking at you." (11:38)

In conclusion, we come to realise by mocking at somebody, we in reality gain no benefit at all.

In one verse Allāh ﷻ says,

وَمِنْ آيَاتِهِ خَلْقُ السَّمٰوَاتِ وَالْأَرْضِ وَاخْتِلَافُ أَلْسِنَتِكُمْ وَأَلْوَانِكُمْ

"From the signs of Allāh is the creation of the heavens and the earth and the differing of your languages (we all speak different dialects and languages) and your colours of skin." (30:22)

In another verse, Allāh ﷻ says,

قُلْ أَبِاللهِ وَآيَاتِهِ وَرَسُوْلِهِ كُنْتُمْ تَسْتَهْزِئُوْنَ

"Say (O Muhammad) are you mocking at Allāh and His signs and His Messenger? (9:65)

لَا تَعْتَذِرُوْا قَدْ كَفَرْتُمْ بَعْدَ اِيْمَانِكُمْ

Do not make any excuses; indeed you have disbelieved after your Imān." (9:66)

Let us now put the first two verses together (verse 30:22 and verse 9:65). What is the outcome and possible punishment of a person who mocks somebody due to their colour or language which is a sign of Allāh's ﷻ greatness, which is immediately mentioned in the next verse (9:66) It will (Allāh ﷻ forbid) make a person go out of the fold of Islām. After uttering such statements, one has to do Tawbah (seek forgiveness), renew their Imān and even renew their marriage. This is how dangerous it can be.

A person once wrote a letter to Shaykh Thānwi ﷺ from Bangladesh. The person was not familiar with the Urdu language so they wrote:

ہم ہنستا ہے

"We laugh in abundance (please give the cure for this excessive laugher)."

Somebody from amongst the gathering heard this, laughed and said in a very sarcastic way, "These people do not even know Urdu properly!" Shaykh Thānwi ﷺ said,

تمہارے ایمان جانے کا خطرہ ہے

"There is a chance of losing your Imān!"

84

We need to realise how serious it is to mock at others especially at their colour of skin and language. In Sūrah Hujurāt, Allāh ﷻ speaks about the respect and honour we should all have for our fellow Muslims and how we should interact with each another.

In the second Rukū of the Sūrah, Allāh ﷻ says,

يَا أَيُّهَا الَّذِينَ اٰمَنُوا لَا يَسْخَرْ قَوْمٌ مِّن قَوْمٍ عَسٰى أَن يَّكُونُوا خَيْرًا مِّنْهُمْ

"O you who have believed, let not one group of people mock at another group of people. It is possible that they (the people being mocked at) are better than them (the people who mock." (49:11)

The word سَخِرَ يَسْخَرُ means to mock or to belittle. Also from this root word, the word تَسْخِيرُ is derived - which means to subjugate or to make somebody lower than yourself. So by mocking at somebody, we are in reality belittling that person which is completely prohibited. The word قَوْمٌ in this verse denotes a group of people in which initially men are mentioned and females are also included within them. Immediately after this verse, Allāh ﷻ addresses the believing women separately and exclusively by saying,

وَلَا نِسَاءٌ مِّن نِّسَاءٍ عَسٰى أَن يَّكُنَّ خَيْرًا مِّنْهُنَّ

"And nor should a group of females mock at another group of females. It is possible that they (i.e. the group of females that are

being mocked at) are better than them (the group of females that are mocking)." (49:11)

In this verse, Allāh ﷻ firstly addresses the believing men. Usually in the Holy Qur'ān, when Allāh ﷻ addresses the believers, He addresses men and women together. For example,

يَا أَيُّهَا الَّذِيْنَ اٰمَنُوْا قُوْا اَنْفُسَكُمْ وَأَهْلِيْكُمْ نَارًا

"O you who have believed, save yourselves and your families from the fire." (66:6)

Within the above verse, both men and women are included. However, in the verse of Sūrah Hujurāt, Allāh ﷻ first mentions the males and then mentions the females separately. The reason for this is to explain the importance and significance of this ruling i.e. of not mocking at each other.

Another reason for this is due to the structure of the Islamic society at that time. Within an Islamic society, segregation was prevalent, hence, men would interact and conduct with men and women would interact and conduct with women.

This verse does not imply or indicate that men can ridicule women or that women can ridicule men. It was because of the societal structure and segregation at that time due to which Allāh ﷻ mentions that men should not mock at another group of men and vice versa, the women folk should not mock at another group of women.

The main root reason for why one mocks at another is because one thinks themself to be superior than the other. He thinks he is better than the other person, therefore they belittle the other person.

The Holy Prophet ﷺ once said in a Ḥadīth narrated by Imām Muslim ﷺ in his Saḥīḥ,

كُلُّ الْمُسْلِمِ عَلَى الْمُسْلِمِ حَرَامٌ دَمُه وَمَالُه وَعِرْضُه بِحَسْبِ امْرِئٍ مِّنَ الشَّرِّ أَنْ يَّحْقِرَ أَخَاهُ الْمُسْلِمَ

"It is forbidden upon every Muslim, another Muslim brothers' blood, wealth and respect. It is sufficient for a person to be considered evil that he belittles his Muslim brother."

Nowadays, when we sit in a gathering, we laugh, chuckle and make fun of people. The Holy Prophet ﷺ said,

فَإِنَّ كَثْرَةَ الضَّحِكِ تُمِيْتُ الْقَلْبَ

"Excessive laughter kills the heart."

Finding Faults

The second significant point Allāh ﷻ mentions in Sūrah Hujurāt is,

وَلَا تَلْمِزُوا أَنْفُسَكُمْ

"Do not insult yourselves." (49:11)

Allāh ﷻ does not say,

وَلَا تَلْمِزُوا بَعْضَكُمْ بَعْضًا

"Let not the Muslims insult one another."

Allāh ﷻ said, "Do not insult yourselves." It is similar to what Allāh ﷻ says in Sūrah Nisā,

وَلَا تَقْتُلُوا أَنْفُسَكُمْ

"Do not kill yourselves." (4:29)

The question arises as to why Allāh ﷻ says, "Do not insult your-selves." The reason is because as Muslims we are all brothers,

إِنَّمَا الْمُؤْمِنُونَ إِخْوَةٌ

"Indeed, all the believers are brothers." (49:10)

The Holy Prophet ﷺ has said,

اَلْمُؤْمِنُوْنَ كَرَجُلٍ وَاحِدٍ إِنِ اشْتَكَى عَيْنُهُ اشْتَكَى كُلُّهُ ، وَإِنِ اشْتَكَى رَأْسُهُ اشْتَكَى كُلُّهُ

"All the believers are like one person. If his eye is in pain, his whole body pains and if his head is in pain, his whole body pains." (Muslim)

This has two meanings:

- By defaming and insulting one Muslim, it is actually abusing the Muslim brotherhood as a whole and thus, this will be completely wrong.

- If an individual insults a Muslim brother e.g. by swearing, then in exchange for that, his Muslim brother will retaliate by swearing back.

A person should also not defame or belittle himself - this is a very important point to remember. Many people become depressed thus downgrade themselves by saying, "I am completely lost, I am an idiot, I am stupid, I am ignorant." A person should not have this attitude but rather, they should keep high hopes and have self esteem. This verse is instructing us not to put ourselves into a low category, so we end up underestimating ourselves.

There are two words in the Arabic language:

1. لُمَزَةٌ

2. هُمَزَةٌ

The word لُمَزَة means defaming a person through words. The word هُمَزَة means defaming a person by action.

Allāh ﷻ says,

وَيۡلٌ لِّكُلِّ هُمَزَةٍ لُّمَزَةٍ

"Destruction to every backbiter, ridiculer." (104:1)

هَمَّازٍ مَّشَّاءٍ بِنَمِيۡمٍ

"A slanderer going about with malicious gossip." (68:11)

The Holy Prophet ﷺ said,

سِبَابُ الۡمُسۡلِمِ فُسُوۡقٌ

"Swearing at another Muslim is transgression." (Muslim)

لَا يَحِلُّ لِمُسۡلِمٍ أَنۡ يُّرَوِّعَ مُسۡلِمًا

"It is not permissible for a believer to frighten another believer." (Tirmizi)

Anything which will cause any kind of disturbance or inconvenience to another believer is also completely impermissible.

اَلۡمُسۡلِمُ مَنۡ سَلِمَ الۡمُسۡلِمُوۡنَ مِنۡ لِسَانِه وَيَدِه

"A true Muslim is he from whose tongue and hand other believers remain safe." (Bukhāri, Muslim)

The Holy Prophet ﷺ did not say مِنْ كَلَامِه (from his speech), he said

مِنْ لِسَانِه (from his tongue). As a sign of disrespect, many young children will stick out their tongue. This is also included in prohibition. Subḥān-Allāh!

Secondly, using the hand is not only confined to slapping or hitting somebody. In this day and age, many people use the excuse, "I did not use my mouth to say anything, I just pressed the button on my mobile." This is included within the definition of وَيَدِه (using the hand). In the early generations, before mobile phones were invented, the scholars could have restricted the clause of وَيَدِه and said it only refers to physical violence. However, by means of social media (Facebook, Twitter, WhatsApp etc.), one will be using their hands, hence this will also be included within the meaning of وَيَدِه.

Bad Nicknames

The third significant point Allāh ﷻ mentions in Sūrah Hujurāt is,

وَلَا تَنَابَزُوا بِالْأَلْقَابِ

"Do not call one other with offensive/bad nicknames." (49:11)

The actual word نَبَزَ means to give bad nicknames. In the beginning stages, a person may have been a drug addict, a gambler or a fornicator. However, the individual then did Tawbah (repented) from their past sins. For another individual to call them with these titles e.g. Fāsiq (transgressor), Kāfir (disbeliever), Zāni (adulterer), drunkard etc. will be completely Harām.

The Holy Prophet ﷺ has said,

اَلتَّائِبُ مِنَ الذَّنْبِ كَمَنْ لَا ذَنْبَ لَه

"A person who has repented from his past sins is like the one who has no sins." (Ibn Mājah)

A person should never expose his Muslim brother or sister's defects by saying things such as, "That person used to be a drug addict and sell alcohol," or "They may be a حَاجِي (Hāji) or مُصَلِّي (Musalli-worshipper) now but I know their past!" This is very dangerous.

If a person disgraces his Muslim brother for something which he has repented from, Allāh ﷻ takes the responsibility upon Himself to disgrace that person in this world. If a person has done Tawbah from fornication and gambling and another individual refers to this person as a gambler, fornicator, adulterer etc. Allāh ﷻ forbid, He takes the responsibility upon Himself that He will disgrace him. He asks, "Why is this person disgracing My servant? He has done Tawbah and I have forgiven him; what rights does this person have to disgrace My servant?"

The Holy Prophet ﷺ said,

لَا تُظْهِرِ الشَّمَاتَةَ لِأَخِيْكَ فَيَرْحَمَهُ اللهُ وَيَبْتَلِيْكَ

"Do not expose happiness over the calamity of your Muslim brother; it is possible Allāh ﷻ will show mercy on him and He will afflict you with the calamity." (Tirmizi)

The word اَلْقَابُ in Arabic means good nicknames. Sometimes, in order to flatter a person in a sarcastic manner, one may say 'Allāmah Sāhib' which is wrong as one is not really meaning it; they are only intending to sarcastically flatter the person. A lot of people remark by saying, "Allāmah Sāhib is coming." Then say, "I meant with the

Alif not the Ayn!" (Allāmah with an Ayn i.e. عَلَّامَةٌ means a person who is very knowledgeable. Allāmah with an Alif i.e. اَلَّامَةُ means a person who gives a lot of pain!)

Sometimes people mock by saying, 'Kāri Sāhib' not 'Qāri' Sāhib' with a Qāf. Kāri with a Kāf i.e. كَارِيْ has no meaning. Qāri' Sāhib with a Qāf i.e. قَارِيْ means a person who recites the Qur'ān with Tajwīd.

The Holy Prophet ﷺ has said,

$$أَنْزِلُوا النَّاسَ مَنَازِلَهُمْ$$

"Treat people according to their individual statuses." (Abū Dāwūd)

We should not give Alqāb (titles) to people when they are not worthy of it; especially if one is saying it in a sarcastic way. This is very despicable and sinful.

Allāh ﷻ says,

$$بِئْسَ الِاسْمُ الْفُسُوْقُ بَعْدَ الْإِيْمَانِ$$

"To accuse a person falsely of a sin after he has accepted Imān is indeed evil." (49:11)

After one has become a believer, using names for people such as Fāsiq (transgressor), Kāfir (disbeliever), Zāni (adulterer), gambler etc is sinful. After accepting Imān, we are all brothers so we should not be calling anyone with these names which he dislikes.

When the Holy Prophet ﷺ came to Madīnah Munawwarah, the people of Ansār had two or three different nicknames. The Holy Prophet ﷺ used to call them with these particular titles. Once a Sahābi ؓ came and said, "Yā Rasūlallāh ﷺ, this person does not like that name," so Allāh ﷻ revealed this verse,

$$ وَلَا تَنَابَزُوا بِالْأَلْقَابِ $$
"Do not call one other with offensive nicknames." (49:11)

The Holy Prophet ﷺ would give honourable titles to his Companions ؓ. Khālid Ibn Walīd ؓ was given the title 'Saifullāh' (The Sword of Allāh ﷻ). Sayyidunā Hamzāh ؓ was given the title 'Asadullāh' (The Lion of Allāh ﷻ). Sayyidunā Abū Bakr ؓ was given the title 'Siddīq' (The Most Truthful) and 'Atīq' (the one who is free from the fire of Jahannam). Sayyidunā Umar ؓ was given the title 'Fārūq' (The one who distinguishes between right and wrong).

Giving good titles is a Sunnah of the Holy Prophet ﷺ. If a person is deserving of that title, we should call them by it. If a person has a nickname which describes them and they cannot be recognised other than with that certain title, as long as one is not using the term in a degrading way, then this is permissible.

For example, many Muhaddithūn (those who are familiar with the science of Hadīth) may occasionally use terms to recognise and distinguish between certain narrators. For example, 'Hamīd At-Tawīl (Hamīd the tall one) is used to differentiate between two Hamīds. Another example is Sulaimān Al-A'mash (Sulaimān the squint eye).

Abdullāh Ibn Mubārak ﷺ was asked, "Can we use the terms tall, squint eye etc. in order to distinguish between certain narrators?" He replied, "If it is with the intention of recognition, for identity, it is permissible, but if it is with the intention of defaming and insulting that person, then it is not permissible."

The Holy Prophet ﷺ himself called a person Dhul-Yadain (a person with who has got lengthy hands). It mentions in the Ahādīth,

اَوْ فِیْ یَدِہٖ طُوْلٌ

"He had long hands."

Going back to the verse, Allāh ﷻ is telling us not to call each other with bad titles; this is the worst type of labelling after Imān. For a person to be named like this is wrong and for an individual to call a person in this way is also wrong.

Allāh ﷻ ends the verse by saying,

وَمَن لَّمۡ يَتُبۡ فَأُوْلَٰئِكَ هُمُ الظَّالِمُوۡنَ

"And whoever does not repent, then such people are the wrong-doers." (49:11)

If a person has perpetrated any of these aforementioned sins, what is the remedy? The answer is present in the above verse; the individual has to perform sincere Tawbah. If one does not repent, then Allāh ﷻ says those people are from the transgressors.

Sūrah Hujurāt is a very distinct Sūrah teaching us the social conduct and etiquettes which we as Muslims must adopt within our family circles, communities, towns and cities. We need to ensure that we use respectable titles when conversing with any elderly person e.g. by saying 'Āp' in urdu.

If this heart that Allāh ﷻ has given us is not purified, then a person will be completely unsuccessful and will be destroyed. So we need to cleanse our hearts from all these different kinds of illnesses.

وَقَدْ خَابَ مَنْ دَسَّاهَا

"And he has failed who pollutes it (the heart)" (91:10)

To begin, let us gain this humility. If we can adopt this humility within our lives, then it will make everything easy for ourselves. To help us, let us remember the prescription that Shaykh Thānwi ﷺ gave: always think to yourself that you are the lowest of the low. Shaykh Thānwi ﷺ says hate the sin not the sinner, hate the فِسْق (Fisq— transgression) not the فَاسِق (Fāsiq—transgressor), hate the كُفْر (Kufr—disbelief) not the كَافِر (Kāfir—disbeliever).

If a person was a Kāfir who was previously committing Kufr, and then brings Imān, the person is forgiven. We despise the sin but not the sinner. We hate the murder not the murderer.

A person may not perform their Salāh which makes us hate them. Shaykh Thānwi ﷺ gives a very beautiful example and says if one's own child has got some black spots or has put some paint or ink over his face, the mother will not say, "I am expelling you out of the house" or "I am throwing you out of the house." No! The mother will never do this. Rather, the mother will clean the child and that child will become beloved to that mother again.

In the same way, if a person does not perform Salāh (prayer), one should say, "Brother, the day you perform your Salāh (prayer),

Māshā-Allāh, you are going to be my beloved. The day you are going to keep the beard, Māshā-Allāh, you are going to be my beloved."

The action that a person does i.e. the sin is wrong. If Allāh ﷻ dislikes the Kāfir, then nobody will be able to accept Imān; nobody would have the ability or strength to accept Imān. Therefore Allāh ﷻ hates the Kufr, Allāh ﷻ does not hate the Kāfir. As Muslims, we need to do the same thing as well; we hate the sin not the sinner.

We have to make a start to work on the heart. Let us think and ponder over the definition of pride—have we got these illnesses and these symptoms present within our hearts? If we have, we must get rid of them.

May Allāh ﷻ give us the true understanding of Dīn and may Allāh ﷻ give us the ability to act upon what has been said.

وَاٰخِرُ دَعْوَانَا أَنِ الْحَمْدُ لِلّٰهِ رَبِّ الْعَالَمِيْنَ

Other titles from JKN Publications

Your Questions Answered

An outstanding book written by Shaykh Mufti Saiful Islām. A very comprehensive yet simple Fatāwa book and a source of guidance that reaches out to a wider audience i.e. the English speaking Muslims. The reader will benefit from the various answers to questions based on the Laws of Islām relating to the beliefs of Islām, knowledge, Sunnah, pillars of Islām, marriage, divorce and contemporary issues.

UK RRP: £7.50

Hadeeth for Beginners

A concise Hadeeth book with various Ahādeeth that relate to basic Ibādāh and moral etiquettes in Islām accessible to a wider readership. Each Hadeeth has been presented with the Arabic text, its translation and commentary to enlighten the reader, its meaning and application in day-to-day life.

UK RRP: £3.00

Du'ā for Beginners

This book contains basic Du'ās which every Muslim should recite on a daily basis. Highly recommended to young children and adults studying at Islamic schools and Madrasahs so that one may cherish the beautiful treasure of supplications of our beloved Prophet ﷺ in one's daily life, which will ultimately bring peace and happiness in both worlds, Inshā-Allāh.

UK RRP: £2.00

How well do you know Islām?

An exciting educational book which contains 300 multiple questions and answers to help you increase your knowledge on Islām! Ideal for the whole family, especially children and adult students to learn new knowledge in an enjoyable way and cherish the treasures of knowledge that you will acquire from this book. A very beneficial tool for educational syllabus.

UK RRP: £3.00

Treasures of the Holy Qur'ān

This book entitled "Treasures of the Holy Qur'ān" has been compiled to create a stronger bond between the Holy Qur'ān and the readers. It mentions the different virtues of Sūrahs and verses from the Holy Qur'ān with the hope that the readers will increase their zeal and enthusiasm to recite and inculcate the teachings of the Holy Qur'ān into their daily lives.

UK RRP: £3.00

Marriage - A Complete Solution

Islām regards marriage as a great act of worship. This book has been designed to provide the fundamental teachings and guidelines of all what relates to the marital life in a simplified English language. It encapsulates in a nutshell all the marriage laws mentioned in many of the main reference books in order to facilitate their understanding and implementation.

UK RRP: £5.00

Pearls of Luqmān

This book is a comprehensive commentary of Sūrah Luqmān, written beautifully by Shaykh Mufti Saiful Islām. It offers the reader with an enquiring mind, abundance of advice, guidance, counselling and wisdom.

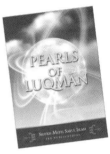

The reader will be enlightened by many wonderful topics and anecdotes mentioned in this book, which will create a greater understanding of the Holy Qur'ān and its wisdom. The book highlights some of the wise sayings and words of advice Luqmān ﷺ gave to his son.

UK RRP: £3.00

Arabic Grammar for Beginners

This book is a study of Arabic Grammar based on the subject of Nahw (Syntax) in a simplified English format. If a student studies this book thoroughly, he/she will develop a very good foundation in this field, Inshā-Allāh. Many books have been written on this subject in various languages such as Arabic, Persian and Urdu. However, in this day and age there is a growing demand for this subject to be available in English .

UK RRP: £3.00

A Gift to My Youngsters

This treasure filled book, is a collection of Islamic stories, morals and anecdotes from the life of our beloved Prophet ﷺ, his Companions ﷺ and the pious predecessors. The stories and anecdotes are based on moral and ethical values, which the reader will enjoy sharing with their peers, friends, families and loved ones.

"A Gift to My Youngsters" – is a wonderful gift presented to the readers personally, by the author himself, especially with the youngsters in mind. He has carefully selected stories and anecdotes containing beautiful morals, lessons and valuable knowledge and wisdom.

UK RRP: £5.00

Travel Companion

The beauty of this book is that it enables a person on any journey, small or distant or simply at home, to utilise their spare time to read and benefit from an exciting and vast collection of important and interesting Islamic topics and lessons. Written in simple and easy to read text, this book will immensely benefit both the newly interested person in Islām and the inquiring mind of a student expanding upon their existing knowledge. Inspiring reminders from the Holy Qur'ān and the blessed words of our beloved Prophet ﷺ beautifies each topic and will illuminate the heart of the reader. **UK RRP: £5.00**

Pearls of Wisdom

Junaid Baghdādī ﷺ once said, "Allāh ﷻ strengthens through these Islamic stories the hearts of His friends, as proven from the Qur'anic verse,
"And all that We narrate unto you of the stories of the Messengers, so as to strengthen through it your heart." (11:120)
Mālik Ibn Dinār ﷺ stated that such stories are gifts from Paradise. He also emphasised to narrate these stories as much as possible as they are gems and it is possible that an individual might find a truly rare and invaluable gem among them. **UK RRP: £6.00**

Inspirations

This book contains a compilation of selected speeches delivered by Shaykh Mufti Saiful Islām on a variety of topics such as the Holy Qur'ān, Nikāh and eating Halāl. Having previously been compiled in separate booklets, it was decided that the transcripts be gathered together in one book for the benefit of the reader. In addition to this, we have included in this book, further speeches which have not yet been printed.

UK RRP: £6.00

Gift to my Sisters

A thought provoking compilation of very interesting articles including real life stories of pious predecessors, imaginative illustrations and much more. All designed to influence and motivate mothers, sisters, wives and daughters towards an ideal Islamic lifestyle. A lifestyle referred to by our Creator, Allāh ﷻ in the Holy Qur'ān as the means to salvation and ultimate success.

UK RRP: £6.00

Gift to my Brothers

A thought provoking compilation of very interesting articles including real life stories of pious predecessors, imaginative illustrations, medical advices on intoxicants and rehabilitation and much more. All designed to influence and motivate fathers, brothers, husbands and sons towards an ideal Islamic lifestyle. A lifestyle referred to by our Creator, Allāh ﷻ in the Holy Qur'ān as the means to salvation and ultimate success.

UK RRP: £5.00

Heroes of Islām

"In the narratives there is certainly a lesson for people of intelligence (understanding)." (12:111)

A fine blend of Islamic personalities who have been recognised for leaving a lasting mark in the hearts and minds of people.

A distinguishing feature of this book is that the author has selected not only some of the most world and historically famous renowned scholars but also these lesser known and a few who have simply left behind a valuable piece of advice to their nearest and dearest. **UK RRP: £5.00**

Ask a Mufti (3 volumes)

Muslims in every generation have confronted different kinds of challenges. In-spite of that, Islām produced such luminary Ulamā who confronted and re-sponded to the challenges of their time to guide the Ummah to the straight path. "Ask A Mufti" is a comprehensive three volume fatwa book, based on the Hanafi School, covering a wide range of topics related to every aspect of human life such as belief, ritual worship, life after death and contemporary legal topics related to purity, commercial transaction, marriage, divorce, food, cosmetic, laws pertaining to women, Islamic medical ethics and much more.

UK RRP: £30.00

Should I Follow a Madhab?

Taqleed or following one of the four legal schools is not a new phenomenon. Historically, scholars of great calibre and luminaries, each one being a specialist in his own right, were known to have adhered to one of the four legal schools. It is only in the previous century that a minority group emerged advocating a se-vere ban on following one of the four major schools.

This book endeavours to address the topic of Taqleed and elucidates its im-portance and necessity in this day and age. It will also, by the Divine Will of Allāh ﷻ dispel some of the confusion surrounding this topic. **UK RRP: £5.00**

Advice for the Students of Knowledge

Allāh ﷻ describes divine knowledge in the Holy Qur'ān as a 'Light'. Amongst the qualities of light are purity and guidance. The Holy Prophet ﷺ has clearly ex-plained this concept in many blessed Ahādeeth and has also taught us many supplications in which we ask for beneficial knowledge.

This book is a golden tool for every sincere student of knowledge wishing to mould his/her character and engrain those correct qualities in order to be wor-thy of receiving the great gift of Ilm from Allāh ﷻ. **UK RRP: £3.00**

Stories for Children

"Stories for Children" - is a wonderful gift presented to the readers personally by the author himself, especially with the young children in mind. The stories are based on moral and ethical values, which the reader will enjoy sharing with their peers, friends, families and loved ones. The aim is to present to the children stories and incidents which contain moral lessons, in order to reform and correct their lives, according to the Holy Qur'ān and Sunnah.

UK RRP: £5.00

Pearls from My Shaykh

This book contains a collection of pearls and inspirational accounts of the Holy Prophet 鷺, his noble Companions, pious predecessors and some personal accounts and sayings of our well-known contemporary scholar and spiritual guide, Shaykh Mufti Saiful Islām Sāhib. Each anecdote and narrative of the pious predecessors have been written in the way that was narrated by Mufti Saiful Islām Sāhib in his discourses, drawing the specific lessons he intended from telling the story. The accounts from the life of the Shaykh has been compiled by a particular student based on their own experience and personal observation. **UK RRP: £5.00**

Paradise & Hell

This book is a collection of detailed explanation of Paradise and Hell including the state and conditions of its inhabitants. All the details have been taken from various reliable sources. The purpose of its compilation is for the reader to contemplate and appreciate the innumerable favours, rewards, comfort and unlimited luxuries of Paradise and at the same time take heed from the punishment of Hell. Shaykh Mufti Saiful Islām Sāhib has presented this book in a unique format by including the Tafseer and virtues of Sūrah Ar-Rahmān. **UK RRP: £5.00**

Prayers for Forgiveness

Prayers for Forgiveness' is a short compilation of Du'ās in Arabic with English translation and transliteration. This book can be studied after 'Du'ā for Beginners' or as a separate book. It includes twenty more Du'ās which have not been mentioned in the previous Du'ā book. It also includes a section of Du'ās from the Holy Qur'ān and a section from the Ahādeeth. The book concludes with a section mentioning the Ninety-Nine Names of Allāh 鷺 with its translation and transliteration. **UK RRP: £3.00**

Scattered Pearls

This book is a collection of scattered pearls taken from books, magazines, emails and WhatsApp messages. These pearls will hopefully increase our knowledge, wisdom and make us realise the purpose of life. In this book, Mufti Sāhib has included messages sent to him from scholars, friends and colleagues which will be beneficial and interesting for our readers Inshā-Allāh. **UK RRP: £4.00**

Poems of Wisdom

This book is a collection of poems from those who contributed to the Al-Mumin Magazine in the poems section. The Hadeeth mentions "Indeed some form of poems are full of wisdom." The themes of each poem vary between wittiness, thought provocation, moral lessons, emotional to name but a few. The readers will benefit from this immensely and make them ponder over the outlook of life in general.

UK RRP: £4.00

Horrors of Judgement Day
This book is a detailed and informative commentary of the first three Sūrahs of the last Juz namely; Sūrah Naba, Sūrah Nāzi'āt and Sūrah Abasa. These Sūrahs vividly depict the horrific events and scenes of the Great Day in order to warn mankind the end of this world. These Sūrahs are an essential reminder for us all to instil the fear and concern of the Day of Judgement and to detach ourselves from the worldly pleasures. Reading this book allows us to attain the true realization of this world and provides essential advices of how to gain eternal salvation in the Hereafter.

RRP: £5:00

Spiritual Heart
It is necessary that Muslims always strive to better themselves at all times and to free themselves from the destructive maladies. This book focusses on three main spiritual maladies; pride, anger and evil gazes. It explains its root causes and offers some spiritual cures. Many examples from the lives of the pious predecessors are used for inspiration and encouragement for controlling the above three maladies. It is hoped that the purification process of the heart becomes easy once the underlying roots of the above maladies are clearly understood.

UK RRP: £5:00

Hajj & Umrah for Beginners
This book is a step by step guide on Hajj and Umrah for absolute beginners. Many other additional important rulings (Masāil) have been included that will Insha-Allāh prove very useful for our readers. The book also includes some etiquettes of visiting (Ziyārat) of the Holy Prophet's 	ﷺ blessed Masjid and his Holy Grave.

UK RRP £3:00

Advice for the Spiritual Travellers
This book contains essential guidelines for a spiritual Murīd to gain some familiarity of the science of Tasawwuf. It explains the meaning and aims of Tasawwuf, some understanding around the concept of the soul, and general guidelines for a spiritual Murīd. This is highly recommended book and it is hoped that it gains wider readership among those Murīds who are basically new to the science of Tasawwuf.

UK RRP £3:00

Don't Worry Be Happy
This book is a compilation of sayings and earnest pieces of advice that have been gathered directly from my respected teacher Shaykh Mufti Saiful Islām Sāhib. The book consists of many valuable enlightenments including how to deal with challenges of life, promoting unity, practicing good manners, being optimistic and many other valuable advices. Our respected Shaykh has gathered this Naseehah from meditating, contemplating, analysing and searching for the gems within Qur'anic verses, Ahādeeth and teachings of our Pious Predecessors. **UK RRP £1:00**

Kanzul Bāri

Kanzul Bāri provides a detailed commentary of the Ahādeeth contained in Saheeh al-Bukhāri. The commentary includes Imām Bukhāri's ﷺ biography, the status of his book, spiritual advice, inspirational accounts along with academic discussions related to Fiqh, its application and differences of opinion. Moreover, it answers objections arising in one's mind about certain Ahādeeth. Inquisitive students of Hadeeth will find this commentary a very useful reference book in the final year of their Ālim course for gaining a deeper understanding of the science of Hadeeth.   **UK RRP: £15.00**

How to Become a Friend of Allāh ﷺ

The friends of Allāh ﷺ have been described in detail in the Holy Qur'ān and Āhadeeth. This book endeavours its readers to help create a bond with Allāh ﷺ in attaining His friendship as He is the sole Creator of all material and immaterial things. It is only through Allāh's ﷺ friendship, an individual will achieve happiness in this life and the Hereafter, hence eliminate worries, sadness, depression, anxiety and misery of this world.   **UK RRP:**

Gems & Jewels

This book contains a selection of articles which have been gathered for the benefit of the readers covering a variety of topics on various aspects of daily life. It offers precious advice and anecdotes that contain moral lessons. The advice captivates its readers and will extend the narrowness of their thoughts to deep reflection, wisdom and appreciation of the purpose of our existence.

End of Time

This book is a comprehensive explanation of the three Sūrahs of Juzz Amma; Sūrah Takweer, Sūrah Infitār and Sūrah Mutaffifeen. This book is a continuation from the previous book of the same author, 'Horrors of Judgement Day'. The three Sūrahs vividly sketch out the scene of the Day of Judgement and describe the state of both the inmates of Jannah and Jahannam. Mufti Saiful Islām Sāhib provides an easy but comprehensive commentary of the three Sūrahs facilitating its understanding for the readers whilst capturing the horrific scene of the ending of the world and the conditions of mankind on that horrific Day.   **UK RRP: £5.00**

Andalus (modern day Spain), the long lost history, was once a country that produced many great calibre of Muslim scholars comprising of Mufassirūn, Muhaddithūn, Fuqahā, judges, scientists, philosophers, surgeons, to name but a few. The Muslims conquered Andalus in 711 AD and ruled over it for eight-hundred years. This was known as the era of Muslim glory. Many non-Muslim Europeans during that time travelled to Spain to study under Muslim scholars. The remanences of the Muslim rule in Spain are manifested through their universities, magnificent palaces and Masājid carved with Arabic writings, standing even until today. In this book, Shaykh Mufti Saiful Islām shares some of his valuable experiences he witnessed during his journey to Spain.   **UK RRP: £3.00**